Daniel T. Broderick III

ISBN-10   1511518626

ISBN-13   978-1511518628

Twenty-five years ago, give or take, I was a young, recently-married girl who first heard about Betty Broderick because someone left a 'People' magazine at my dentist's office.

There she was on the cover, young – even younger than I was then – wearing an old-fashioned lace and tulle wedding dress, and so beautiful!

She was gazing at the photographer with this hopeful little smile on her stunning face, and seated next to her was this kind of weird-looking guy, dressed in this sad looking getup, and they didn't seem like they belonged together at all.

The picture made me curious enough about why these two were on the cover that I picked up the issue and started to read. Five minutes later, I waved off my doctor's annoyed receptionist when she called my name. I was hooked and I'm still hooked, and that's how I came to know Betty.

But that meeting lay decades into the future. On that day, I sympathized only with Linda Kolkena Broderick – Betty's ex-husband Dan's lover and second wife – so young, so pretty. She could have been me, killed senselessly at the height of all the power and possibilities that come from being young and beautiful and newly married to a powerful handsome older man.

See, that's the thing about Betty's story: At one time or another we're all going to go there somehow.

That day, when I opened the magazine, all I saw with all the shocked judgment of a twenty-five year old girl who could eat a large pizza and easily slide into my size four dresses at 5'10", was a woman who had let herself go to hell and lost a pretty hot-looking man to a younger, thinner woman, a winner of a woman, and Betty ... well, Betty was clearly no winner.

I sighed in righteous disgust and made a mental note to myself to buy any books written on her.

I did, and I watched the made-for-TV movies too. *Eek*, I said to myself, *what a witch, what a psycho, that poor couple ...* I read the magnificent 'Until the Twelfth of Never' and shuddered for Dan and Linda's travails. *My God!*

I chatted to my girlfriends. What else could they have done besides lie and sneak around? I mean, she was so crazy and they were so in love, and really it was all her fault because she did look terrible after she cut her hair and gained weight, and well, you know...uhm, got old like that.

Remember, that was back in the day. We didn't know much about adultery, how it hits you like a bucket of battery acid and destroys your brain and sears your heart. There was no Clara Harris driving a Mercedes over and over (and over) her cheating husband. Back then, all astronauts were simply heroes and not diaper-wearing, pepper-spraying, would-be assassins, like Lisa Nowak. There was no beautiful doctor running around kicking in dog doors and scattering condoms at her rival's house, like Dr. Siler-Fisher.

All these stories, all our own stories of heartache and madness, were ahead of us. At that more innocent time there was only Betty, "a woman in ruins," as the late, great Bella Stumbo once said, and none of us wanted to ever, ever, think that might – could ever be – us.

Oh, but she is. Betty is everywoman, everywoman who ever loved and lost and didn't simply go home and either eat herself into a coma or lay in the bathtub eyeing her razor longingly. She was us at the outer edges of our worst despair, of our most maddening, senseless angers and the terrible acts that anger sometimes draws.

I grew up, got old, became a writer, and got to know Betty, and she became a friend. I like her. Anyone who ever met her would. She's smart, and kind, and funny, and vulnerable, and lonely, and hurt, and hopeful. She's in each of us and represents both the best and worst things that being a woman can mean, that being a woman can bring.

This is her story in her own words. I hope you'll enjoy getting to hear from her as much as I have.

Kathleen McKenna Hewtson
San Francisco, 2015

The Summer Day

Who made the world?
Who made the swan, and the black bear?
Who made the grasshopper?
This grasshopper, I mean—
the one who has flung herself out of the grass,
the one who is eating sugar out of my hand
who is moving her jaws back and forth instead of up and down—
who is gazing around with her enormous and complicated eyes.
Now she lifts her pale forearms and thoroughly washes her face.
Now she snaps her wings open, and floats away.
I don't know exactly what a prayer is.
I do know how to pay attention, how to fall down
into the grass, how to kneel down in the grass,
how to be idle and blessed, how to stroll through the fields,
which is what I have been doing all day.
Tell me, what else should I have done?
Doesn't everything die at last, and too soon?
Tell me, what is it you plan to do
with your one wild and precious life?

Mary Olive

Chapter 1

IT TAKES TWO

It always takes two.

It takes two to fall in love, hold hands, and to kiss.

It takes two to develop a private language of inside jokes.

It takes two to slow-dance to your favorite songs.

It takes two to get married, be married, and stay married.

It takes two to argue and make up, over and over.

It takes two on the see-saw of life, where one is up and the other down, but if you try real hard, and breathe just right, you can make it balance for a long time. That's the real fun.

But it only takes one to kill, to go to a house, to climb the stairs, to find in bed the two people who have angered you for years, who have humiliated you without mercy, who have tortured you, who have brought you so low with their psychological games that you hardly recognize yourself, who have destroyed your life and then destroyed it again, over and over, remorselessly, who have taken everything from you – your children, your self-respect, your financial security, your home, any sense you have of yourself, any sense of your own decency and worth – to the point that you believe they must be trying to kill you or why else would they be doing this?

Stupid Betty, Ugly Betty, Crazy Betty, Useless Betty.

You are standing there with your gun, not intending to use it, just trying to get a little power back into your relationship, to make them *stop!*

Then something happens ... she lunges forward. Life takes over. And death takes over. You are, after all, the one holding the gun.

That is why I am here. That is why I have been in prison for twenty-five years. Because I killed them when all my grief, all my torment, all my anger, all my shame, all my desolation came tumbling down. And life overtook me. Death overtook me. My sanity ...

Do I feel guilty? In my 2010 parole hearing, I said that I should not have killed them. Of course I should not have killed them. What I did was inexcusable. All killing is wrong, in war and in peace, in anger and in cold blood. But when you are trying to save yourself, maybe it is explicable: *If you don't control them, they will control you.* It is the logic of warfare, and a divorce is the closest most of us will come to war in our civilian lives. There is us ... and there is the enemy. My enemy. And sometimes, in the worst domestic circumstances, it comes down to 'control or be controlled.'

And at that moment, life takes over; the desire to live and the necessity of ... I don't know what. And, as in battle, the reason why you are in this predicament is lost. There is just you and him ...

I shot Daniel T. Broderick III because I wanted to survive, to live,

10

far more than I wanted him to die. In the heat of battle, I let rip.

And Linda Broderick – Linda Kolkena, as I always think of her – why did she have to die? Cruel as she was to me, she wasn't really my enemy. She was just there. She just happened to be at the end of the gun I wanted to use to have some control over Dan, to say that I was somebody, a human being, a loving, kind human being, who had wanted only the best for both of us, for him, for me, for our children – Kim, Lee, Danny and Rhett. And now I was nothing, less than nothing, a figment of the court's imagination, a cypher, a has-been, a somebody who was now a nobody, worthless, futile, superfluous.

To be me again, Dan had to be put into context – not to die, but certainly to be taught to leave me alone.

And in a few seconds, I let every pain, every cruelty, every sadness, every hurt and every abuse take me over. It only took a few seconds to define me.

Then Linda was dead. Then Dan was dead. I never wanted Dan dead. I loved him. He was my measure of myself, the man I had loved, and admired, and in many ways served, for twenty years.

But life takes us all over occasionally, and on some occasions the result is catastrophic, irredeemable, irreparable, beyond rescuing or excuse.

This is what I wanted to explain during my two trials for first degree murder in 1990 and 1991. This is what I wanted to explain

11

during my parole hearing in 2010. This is what those juries at least partially understood when they could come to no verdict in my first trial and acquitted me of first degree murder in my second. I don't think the parole board understood me at all because it wanted me to say there was no reason for what I did.

But there was a reason. There were a thousand reasons. Just no excuses.

So that is what I said, and it wasn't enough.

The title of this book came from my years in the battered women's group in prison, here at Chino-Corona in California. Every time any of the women talked about all the terribly abusive things their partners did to them, all I kept thinking was: *why?*

Why did you allow it? Why did you stay? Why in the world didn't you leave him?

I guess that is what everyone thinks whenever they hear a story about abuse.

There's an immediate judgment, and I believe now that judgment comes with a little feeling of, 'Not me. It could never happen to me, and if it did, if somehow it did, why then I'd leave. I'd do this, or that, I'd do anything but stick around. But then why am I even thinking of these ugly things, because it couldn't ever happen to me anyway?'

From there we shrug it off and go back to our lives. We can even manage to do that if it is happening to us, because *it isn't, it couldn't be, I'm not that kind of woman, he's not that kind of man, it's not the kind of relationship I could ever be in,* even if it's exactly the kind of relationship we are in.

The answers to how you end up there are many and complicated. Or maybe not, maybe that's just another thing I told myself; because my own life story seemed impossible to compare to anyone else's. It did then, it doesn't now.

I suppose it depends on who you are in the relationship, your self-esteem, your values, your sense of what you are worth and his sense of those things too, because it always takes two to make any relationship what it is, for good or evil.

From the very beginning of my relationship with Dan, there were red flags and alarms which I either failed to notice or chose to ignore. I didn't know anything about abuse in those days.

I was not a sophisticated child. I was raised in a very strict, sheltered Catholic home and had little life experience.

I met Dan in 1965, when I was seventeen. I was a very friendly, trusting, 'good' girl, who always wanted to do the right thing and make my parents happy by being a credit to them.

I have learned so many things in prison that I never knew before. I learned the 'The Warning Signs of an Abuser,' and that all abuse is

13

about power and control. I have learned that alcoholism, such as Dan's, is a progressive disease and the cure is not as simple as just saying, "Stop drinking, why don't you?"

I guess it will sound strange saying this, but it's honest all the same. Prison has opened my eyes to so many true things. I went from very strict, protective parents, directly into the arms of a very strict, controlling husband, without one single day on my own where I could have made my own choices and tried to live my own life. I never thought about what I was missing then, because you can't miss what you've never had, or at least that's what I used to believe.

Of course, I guess it's true also that a life like that – protected, controlled – can have its privileges. I didn't have to worry about paying the rent, taxes, insurances, and whatever else. But it's also like binding the feet of women in China to keep them from learning to walk on their own, or at least to walk very far.

I'm sorry to go to another analogy but I've had a long time to think in here and now that I'm writing I have a lot to get across. For a caged bird, it doesn't matter in the end how nice, or even gilded, the cage is, that bird can't fly and all she's really doing is living in a place that, despite appearances, is a prison and marking down time to a slow death from a life that was never lived at all.

From the outside, by people looking in at me in my cage, I was envied, maybe even admired, but I wanted to fly. I thought, if given a chance, I might even soar.

But I didn't get a chance and I didn't get to soar.

The unique, and I hope for your sake, brilliant tapestry of this one life of ours is formed every day by the experiences we have now and the ones that have come before. This is who we are, and it's not so much even what actually happens to us that matters as how we feel about it and how it affects what we do, how we react.

I'm where I am because of my reactions to events based on how I felt and understood them while they were happening to me during a period of utter, spiraling despair. I don't know if any of it will make sense, or even be interesting, to people, but what the heck, it's my life and it's a true story.

"Big, bad Betty."

"Betty get your gun."

"One angry Betty."

Somebody suggested the death of Dan and Linda should spawn a, "Be nice to your ex-wife day."

These are just a few of the hundreds of things people have said and written about me, but mostly I guess they just agree with Oprah Winfrey when she shook her head, sighed soulfully into the camera, and said, "Betty, Betty, Betty."

Yep, that's me, Betty Broderick. I'm the woman who became

15

instantly famous for killing her ex-husband and his second wife. I've been the subject of books, blogs, some over-the-top made-for-TV movies, and countless articles.

If the letters I receive to this day are any indication, I'm still the subject of armchair psychologists, who sift the evidence, weigh the pros and cons, and come to their considered conclusions, and of fellow victims of marital abuse, usually women, who would have liked to have done to their spouses what I did to mine.

From where I sit – and in case anyone has forgotten, that's in the California Institution for Women out here in the farmland around Chino-Corona – I don't feel all that interesting, or not interesting enough anyway to write a book about my life. But I've done it anyway, on the off-chance that my life and experiences will offer some insights into how things can go as wrong as wrong can be, or more realistically, if that doesn't work, then maybe it will just be some decent entertainment for readers. Either way is good by me.

What most people experiencing difficulties don't realize, or want to realize early enough to avoid screwing up, is that they're just going on with their lives, coping with their circumstances, rather than using their minds to control the effects their circumstances are having on them. This is another one of the fabulous things I've learned in prison that I really didn't know before. I was stuck merely coping, and I didn't think about why I did what I did, or how I'd gotten to where I was, or how to change it. I just reacted to whatever happened to me.

Chapter 2

NEW YORK, NEW YORK

As a very young child, I had to develop some strong coping strategies for the first ten years of my life.

I was my parents' third child, with two siblings ahead of me and two more to come. This inherited position put me right smack in the middle of everything. I wasn't the oldest, nor was I the youngest; I wasn't the first girl nor the baby girl; I wasn't part of the older pair, nor was I one of the younger pair. I felt lost and alone, doing the best I could amid the chaos of the post-war 'Baby Boom' era, a period of history that saw dramatic social changes taking place.

My mother was from the Bronx, New York, and like a lot of young girls in the early Forties, she married her handsome young soldier before he went off to war to find either glory or death – fighting first in Italy and then in North Africa, in my dad's case. While she waited for him to return, she moved in with her parents, as Dan's mother did with hers.

My grandpa, Michael Cutler, was a six-foot-four, handsome, Irish NYPD detective, and my grandmother, Mary Alice Cutler, was a schoolteacher. They had two daughters: my mother, Marita, and her sister, my Aunt Catherine. Both girls graduated from Hunter College

18

with high hopes and both became teachers, like their mother before them.

My mom was a city girl. She loved everything about it: the shows, the parks, the libraries and museums, and the mass transit system of New York that took her to all the places she wanted to go.

While living with her parents and her sister in that large old apartment building, named Hope Place, in the Bronx, she gave birth to my sister Marita-Jane. The whole family adored that first baby.

My mother never allowed my dad to tell any of us about his war experiences. I never understood why. I think he would have liked to have shared his stories with his children.

My dad was also born in New York and spoke both English and Italian because both his parents were from Italy and spoke Italian to him at home. My mother, who was Irish, was not interested in learning Italian herself, and did not allow him to share his Italian language with us any more than his war stories. To this day I wish I knew how to speak Italian.

My dad's family lived in Westchester County. Unlike Mom, he was not a city kid. He was used to, and liked, lots of land and open fields around him, and those large houses and cars that usually accompanied such places, at least in the wilds of Westchester.

My dad left college to go to war and by the time he got back everything he knew about America had changed. I think this is when the upheaval in our family started, when Dad came home, and he and my mom took an apartment across the hall from her parents.

As both of them were good Catholics, my mom got pregnant again right away in 1946, this time with my brother Frank, and then with me in 1947, putting pressure on my dad to find a job, and in a hurry.

My dad was the youngest of six and his family was in the plastering business. All his older brothers were doing very well working on homes, suburban schools, hospitals, corporate centers and the newly-emerging shopping centers, so it made sense for my dad to join them. This meant moving to the brand new suburbs that were being built for the young post-war families, forcing my mom to leave her city. My dad, however, found himself right at home again. He was used to cars and driving. My mother wasn't and she refused driving lessons and showed not the slightest interest in learning how to drive, at least until after all her children were grown and gone.

After they moved to the suburbs, my mother immediately had two more children in quick succession – my sister Clare and my brother Gerard – so there were soon the seven of us living on Joyce Road in Eastchester, New York.

My mother's only sibling, her sister Catherine, married and also moved to Joyce Road, a few houses down on the same side of the street as us. She had four children at almost the exact same time as my

20

mother, and my four cousins were like my extended family of brothers and sisters.

Every house in the neighborhood was the same – families with kids. I remember a happy childhood, I think we all do. In a lot of ways it's still the same on Joyce Drive. My Uncle Al and his youngest daughter, Marianne, still live in their original house there at number 8. My Uncle is ninety-nine now.

We were more crowded in our house than at my aunt and uncle's because we had more kids. My dad eventually built on extensions but we were in really tight quarters for those first years and my mother was in way over her head, raising five kids and living in suburbia.

Her own stubborn choice not to learn to drive made her very isolated and bored. Her time was filled with endless and repetitive housework and laundry, and I think she was one of the original Desperate Housewives. She had her sister close by but she missed the pace of city life and all the interesting things that were readily available to her in New York. There was no mass transit station for her on every corner in the suburbs and she was basically a woman who was deeply unhappy with the life she had chosen, or at least drifted into, by taking on the traditional role of wife and mother. I don't think she ever blamed herself for where she was, though; that burden she placed on my father, and he got the brunt of her misery and complaining because he 'had moved her out of her element,' and 'loaded her up' with so many kids so fast.

In consequence, my dad spent years paying for what my mother saw as his crimes against her, having to work all day and then come home to do the grocery shopping and drive all of us wherever we needed to go, because, no matter what, my mother remained unrelenting in her refusal to learn to drive. My Aunt Catherine drove and got out a lot more because of it. Aunt Catherine, or "Aunt Cay" as I called her, was a much happier woman – not always on the edge, like my own mother – and I spent as much time as I could at her house.

I was always afraid of my mother's anger. Ever since I was very little, her screaming and yelling frightened me, leaving me with a strong desire to please everyone. From an early age I learned how to walk on eggshells and to disappear from view, even if I was in the same room as my mom, all designed to avoid being the target of her rage. It was the perfect training for anyone aspiring to excel in the future as a doormat and a victim.

My saving grace came in the form of another baby, born when I was ten years old, in 1957. Many of the women back then had a 'caboose baby' as they neared forty. Maybe they still do, I don't know. They did it because they didn't want to go to work. By then their initial brood was away at school all day, so they had to do something to justify their staying home all day.

Dan's mother, meantime, was doing the exact same thing in

Pittsburgh. On the surface it seemed as though Dan and I had very similar, even parallel, childhoods but there were some critical differences that would show up to challenge us throughout our lives together.

Dan was the oldest in his family. He was the king of the hill, the one who was born to comfort his mother for his father's absence while he was away at war and to give his father something amazing, *someone* amazing, to come home to, his firstborn son, his son and heir – or rather his *sun and air* – because that is basically who Dan was to his parents, and at least from where I sat, to each of his numerous younger siblings as well. Starting out life as a firstborn son gave him a distinct advantage and confidence that served him well always. I had no such inborn advantage and for a long, long time all I wanted was to be invisible and to be left in peace.

Back in Eastchester, I immediately took over the care of the new baby. At the age of ten I became an expert in diapering, feeding, burping and everything else to do with a newborn's needs. It was great. Ten is an awkward age anyhow – you are too big for dolls and not yet a teenager – so I finally found my niche in childcare, and in pleasing my mom, and it gave me something to do at the beach club all summer long.

The other mothers took notice and started asking me to watch their kids too. Pretty soon I had a little childcare service going

23

underneath the shade of the large oak tree on the lawn, while my mom and her friends sat in a big circle of chairs on the beach and enjoyed the sun and the sand. Word spread fast at the club that I was experienced, competent and good with kids, and always available to babysit. That I was also only ten didn't seem to bother anyone as far as my burgeoning employability went.

We went to Catholic schools right from grammar straight through to college. Back at Immaculate Conception Grammar School I had a good friend named Aileen. Her mother worked in the church rectory. One day a call came in to the rectory from a young Catholic couple who had just moved into the area. They were looking for a reliable babysitter for their little girls, and Aileen's mother sent her daughter over to be their babysitter. Aileen did not enjoy babysitting, so she recommended me for the job. Thus began one of the happiest periods of my life; another thread in my tapestry, if you will.

I was only twelve, so I was too young to have a 'real' job yet, but I was available every day after school and on weekends. The Finks lived in a tiny little house in Tuckahoe near my school and I could walk there. They were among the best and the nicest people I've ever met. The mother, Mrs. Fink, was beautiful and she had graduated from a Catholic college, Rosemont, to marry a nice Catholic boy who had attended Notre Dame, as Dan would in years to come.

The Finks had two little girls and she was already pregnant with their third baby. I came every day at 3pm and stayed until about 7pm. The dad was a lawyer and took the evening train home from Manhattan. I don't know if his job or his commute stressed him out; all I saw was a man who walked in through the door with a smile and a hello kiss for his wife and kids. Then he'd roll up his sleeves and help me feed, bathe and get the children into bed. Their family became my role models for a happy life, much more so than my own parents.

Betty with R. Fink Jr.

I stayed a part of the Fink family all through my high school and into my college years. They ended up having three more children, all boys. Like my real family, they outgrew their small house and moved to a much larger home. They relied on my help, and I relied on their love and acceptance and kindness. I loved their kids, too, and worked hard to play with them and keep them safe and clean and fed, and in return they trusted and valued me.

In high school I would take a different bus home and go directly to their house. I wanted to be there much more than I wanted to go out on teenage dates. It was the same on weekends. By thirteen I was also doing some modeling, which started when I was drafted by my mom to wear a dress in a church fashion show. I was already five foot eleven by then and I was extremely thin.

As a little kid, being so tall and pale and thin and different-looking was a bad thing in my family, but when I turned thirteen all of a sudden being blond and tall and thin became the best thing possible. I was the proverbial family ugly duckling who turned into a swan for a while.

So for that church fashion show I wore a particular dress because there was no one else in the parish that could fit into it. I remember it perfectly: it was handmade Irish lace on top, with an emerald green moiré silk skirt. In the heels my mother gave me, I was well over six feet tall and the dress was the last and most dramatic in the show. It

26

launched my modeling career, although I had to get underage working papers and I couldn't drive yet. Back then stores were only open in the evenings on Thursdays, so I started working Thursday evenings and Saturdays at Bonwit Teller in White Plains before they opened their big new store in Scarsdale, right near my home.

So during that time I went to high school, got good grades and had two jobs. If I wasn't at Bonwit's, I was at the Finks' house, taking care of their kids. I preferred to stay busy and I liked both of my jobs. Then I got a third job and a fourth job, and it was all pretty crazy, but I made a lot of money and I enjoyed each of them.

My older sister was a hostess at the huge new Schafft's restaurant in the same shopping center as the new Bonwit's, and I got a job there too. Schafft's was open every night and on weekends, and I put in a lot of hours. I was still doing Bonwit's on Thursdays and Saturdays, and during the summer I ran a day camp for kids at a local public school where I worked from 8am till noon. Then I went to Schafft's, and sometimes Bonwit's, and off to the Finks whenever they needed me. Suddenly I was sixteen and preparing for college, and I had saved up plenty of money and bought myself a little green convertible MG in cash.

My relationship with my mother wasn't very good at that time. As a 'good' mother, she always wanted to know where I was and what I was doing. I always told her but she always refused to believe me. I didn't smoke or do drugs, and I didn't take the pill or even have a date in high school. It didn't matter; she was always yelling at me and accusing me of things.

Like most teenagers, I thought my mother was crazy. I guess she was trying to protect me, but all I know is that I never wanted to be at home. Working was my only escape from an unhappy home life and there were other bonuses: I felt competent and valued when I was working, and I made money too. When it came time to pick a college, I chose Mount Saint Vincent's because it was Catholic, like me, and it had a beautiful, lush, scenic campus right on the banks of the Hudson River. It was also close enough to Manhattan to keep my jobs at Bonwit's, the Finks' and Schafft's, and besides my mother didn't encourage us to go away to college. If we had she would have lost control over us, and to be fair, with four of us in college at the same time, the expenses would have gone through the roof if we all went away for school.

Frank, my closest sibling, went to Manhattan College, which was the boys' school for Mount Saint Vincent in the same way that Saint Mary's was the girls' school for Notre Dame back in the Sixties. My two sisters, Marita and Clare, went to Marymount in Manhattan, but I never thought of going there. I wanted a real campus and Marymount was in a series of Brownstones, so Mount Saint Vincent's was perfect for me, and my little car gave me a lot of freedom to come and go.

Chapter 3

DANIEL THOMAS BRODERICK III

Dan's early life was similar to mine in many ways. His mother went home to Duluth, Minnesota, to live with her mother while her husband went off to war. Her new husband, Daniel Broderick II, was from Pittsburgh. His family had a lumber business which, like my family's plastering company, also did very well in the post-war building boom.

The Brodericks also had their own baby boom back home in Pittsburgh when Dan II came home, with Yolanda, Dan's mother, giving birth to another six children right after the war, and then a couple more after that, bringing the total to nine. As in my family, all of them attended Catholic schools. Dan's dad worked in the family business and his mom stayed home raising the children.

As I have said, many things in our two households were similar but a few important things were very different. Dan's father ran the family completely. He held the purse strings and made every decision, both small and large. He was also a heavy drinker who eventually graduated into being a full-blown, drunken wife-abuser. In our household, my mother ran the family and neither of my parents drank at home. These were important differences that I failed to see as the warning signals they should have been. Besides, Dan didn't like his father and he hated the way he drank and treated his mother and the kids as a result. He was adamant that he was never going back to Pittsburgh because he didn't feel comfortable around his dad.

Looking back, I see that we met at the perfect time because we were each trying to break away from our fairly overpowering childhood homes and forge our own paths. We both had big dreams for our futures. We were both young and healthy and accomplished, and very much in love, when we married in 1969. But we had gotten our wires crossed, I understand that now, now that it's way too late to make anything different from our lives. Dan wanted to marry someone like his mother and I wanted to marry a man like my father, or even better like Bob Fink. It's pretty natural for young people to idealize and compartmentalize people and their futures into what seems right and good to them. Dan and I did have a lot in common but I was nothing like his mother and he was nothing like my dad, the family man.

Chapter 4

COLLEGE DAZE 1965-1969

I entered college as a freshman in 1965.

Starting college is scary for anyone, all those new people and places. And yes, it's exhilarating to be on your own for the first time, but scary nonetheless. There was no homeroom anymore and the classes were in different buildings, and there was nobody to make sure you showed up in the right place at the right time.

Worse – or better, depending on how you look at it – nobody even cared if you failed or passed. You were on your own.

I felt ready for it, though. I thought I was smart enough for the work and I had my little sports car and a wardrobe of clothes to die for from working all those years in one of the most upscale stores in America. By sixteen I owned a pair of real Gucci shoes, Natori silk and satin monogrammed lingerie, and Hermès scarfs, and from my mother, who no matter what else made sure that we had the best of everything, there were pearls from Tiffany's and lots of really good quality gold jewelry. At least when it came to the trimmings of life, I felt ready.

Back then, Catholic schoolgirls were wearing uniforms all the way through high school, and when we got to college there was also a uniform we were all expected to wear. It consisted of Villager shirt waist dresses, with small prints and cashmere cable knit sweaters in contrasting pastels, and on our feet a pair of delicate Capezio ballet flats.

In the winters we wore plaid skirts and cashmere cardigans with scarves, and I knew exactly how to dress for my time and place in the world. I think I always looked pretty good. My hair was very long back then and I loved to laugh and to dance, and if I looked happy all the time, it's because I was ... then. Life had yet to hand me down any tragedies or real struggles, and I thought if I followed the rules, and got good grades, and always did the right thing, my future would be perfect.

By the time I was at college, we had moved from Eastchester and Joyce Street to Bronxville, which was, and is, a very affluent suburb of New York. It seemed like every kid there had sports cars and nice clothes, and all of us attended good schools, and nobody appeared to have a worry in the world. The shadow over the country at that time was the Vietnam War, but none of the rich kids in Bronxville was concerned about getting drafted. They knew their daddies would make sure that didn't happen.

I made a lot of nice new friends at college. We had a welcoming afternoon tea dance in September of 1965 and there I met another tall girl like myself, another Aileen. She had a brother, Bill, who was a senior at Notre Dame in South Bend, Indiana. That was a championship year for Notre Dame football and their big rival was U.S.C. Bill invited me to join him in Indiana for the USC/ND football weekend, and since I'd never been to anything like that, I happily said yes. I was accompanied by another girl and we were well chaperoned, as was mandatory in the Sixties for 'good' girls.

Bill took care of everything and we had a fabulous time. The campus was blazing with fall colors and the sun was shining. In those days, the old field house was still in use for the pre-game pep rally the night before and there was a seniors-only party off campus at the Indiana Club. Jerry Lee Lewis himself was right next to me banging out 'Great Balls of Fire.' It was very crowded and noisy in there; it wasn't my kind of party. I had been brought up to be a very proper young lady, which translated into no smoking, no drinking and being highly nervous around boys. My mother had seen to all that. She had also ensured that I was always prepared for any emergency, an emergency in those days translating into any of the above situations occurring. So, as a just in case, I always carried a small purse with ten dollars cash for a cab and a handkerchief, as well as a silver Tiffany pen. Armed with these items against vice, I was ready for anything, or so I thought.

I guess my little pen is the reason I met Daniel T. Broderick III in

33

the first place. He came over and sat at our table and asked if anyone had a pen. Raised for cooperation, I said, "I do," and gave him mine, and with it he wrote his name right there on the white linen tablecloth,

Daniel T. Broderick, III M.D. (A)

I looked at that bold signature and then at him, and asked him the only question I could think of, "What's the 'A' for?"

He answered back that it stood for 'almost,' and then began to tell me that he had applied to both law school and medical school, and that he had just been accepted to Cornell Medical School in New York.

I said, "Oh, I'm from New York!"

He said, "Great, I'll look you up when I get there."

Well, I knew that Cornell was in Ithaca, New York, and so there was no chance I'd ever see him again. It was just another hello and goodbye thing, like I'd been doing all weekend with other girls and guys who were there from all over the United States. That whole weekend had been nothing but non-stop, crowded parties and we all had so much fun.

Bill was a great escort and when I left for home I never gave another thought to the bold young guy who'd signed his name on the tablecloth. I had my jobs and my studies and parties, and, finally, I was making time for dates with all the new college guys I met through my friends. It was a carefree, fun time, exactly like college and life are supposed to be at seventeen.

Then flowers started coming, and telegrams. It seemed that Dan Broderick was coming to the Notre Dame/Navy game and wanted to meet me at Grand Central Station. I'd never met a guy on a street corner and I wasn't planning to start, so I refused. But my employer and idol Bob Fink told me I had to go and gave me a full-length Raccoon coat from his own Notre Dame days to wear. I have always loved Notre Dame football because of Bob Fink. He was a huge fan and always talked about it and gave me tickets to Notre Dame events.

My mother encouraged me to go to the game too, saying, "Go. You'll have fun and he might have some tall friends you can meet." I suppose most Catholic school kids stick together – we're encouraged to – and certainly my mother always wanted me to go to the Notre Dame dances and concerts and parties when they were held in the big New York hotels.

So I did it. I went to the game and I looked great. Like the party I'd met him at, the game was noisy and crowded, and I thought Dan was cute, but he wasn't my type. I always dated tall athletes because I was tall and I liked to wear heels when I went out, and I would only date guys whom I thought were suitable for marriage. Marriage seemed to be the only plan back then. No matter your education or ambitions, marriage was it. Given that, I had a list in my head: My as-yet-imaginary husband must be Catholic and college-educated and ambitious. These were the items on my little invisible check list, but I think every girl has always had those. I didn't like smokers or drinkers, because drunken boys scared me. I liked to feel protected by a guy and wanted my escorts to take care of me on our dates. If they got drunk or smoked, I didn't go out with them a second time.

It turns out that Dan had told all of his friends, "See that girl over there ...? That's the girl I'm going to marry."

He'd said it the night we first met in South Bend, so him getting me to agree to go with him to the Navy game was both a coup and a validation of his pulling power. He wanted to show me off in front of all of his geeky friends, and I didn't disappoint him ... or them. It was a fun day but no big deal to me. Of course I thought about marriage, but way down the road. I had just started college.

However, it was different for the guys in their junior college years at that time because of Vietnam and the draft. Married men did not get drafted, so marriage was a big deal, even a necessity.

It wasn't that way for me, though. I wasn't taking any boy seriously in 1965. 'Girls Just Wanna Have Fun' was my motto many years before Cyndi Lauper turned it into what became my favorite song. There was plenty of time later for marriage and kids; all the time in the world, it seemed, from the perspective of being seventeen.

Yes, I did want to be married eventually to a handsome, successful man whom I loved and who loved me in return. I wanted the nice-looking life my parents had, with beautiful homes and cars, and good furniture, clothes, trips, and country clubs, and I was sure when the time came that I would have all of that. But not right then, not yet.

When Dan arrived at Cornell University Medical School – on the corner of 69th and York Avenue in NYC – in the September of 1966, he wanted us to get together right away. I wasn't so anxious to do that, so I sent a college friend of mine, Marianne, to meet him instead. He was furious at me. Marianne was a smoker and he hated smokers, so I told him I was sorry, and because I felt bad about it, I said that I guessed I could drive down to the city and meet him there. Dan had never lived in New York and he had no friends or family there, and he didn't have a car, and he didn't know his way around the city, whereas I did.

I picked him up in my little MG and I let him drive, telling him that we were going to head up to West Side Drive to hook up with a bunch of my friends from Mount Saint Vincent's. All of a sudden he pulled my car over to the side of the road and turned off the key. Turning to me, he said, "Let's get something straight right now. You do not tell me where we are going or what we are doing!"

37

I felt shocky and just said, "Oh, I'm so sorry. I didn't mean to be bossy. It's just that you don't know anyone here, so I thought you might like to get together with my friends."

Talk about a bunch of warning signs, bells, whistles and alarms. If I'd known then what I know now, I would have, and should have, told him to get out of my car and left him there. But no, I apologized to him. Duh! Which was what he was expecting me to do. In his household, the males had complete power and control over the females, and that was Dan's only model of how to be a man.

Still, we forgave each other and we had a lot of fun together after that. He was cute, he was smart, he was a good dresser and he was really witty. Dating in Manhattan is magical anyway, and we did so many great things. Times Square and Broadway were the epicenter of our world and we saw a lot of theater and movies, and spent time in Central Park and Washington Square and all the clubs in Greenwich Village. Then we developed a group of Medical student friends and we used to hang out with them at Hennies Bar. It became like a second home to us.

Meanwhile I was still in college, going to classes full-time and working several jobs. I was the one with the car and the money and the friends and the big family in New York, and Dan wanted to marry me right away.

I laughed at him.

Despite this, he told his mother in Pittsburgh that he had found the girl he was going to marry and so she flew up to New York to check me out. I passed inspection but it didn't matter because I adamantly refused to get married before I had graduated from college in three years' time.

Dan tried to convince me that I could do both: be married and attend college full-time.

I said, "No way. When I get married I want to give it my all. I don't want to do either marriage or college halfway."

I stuck to that decision no matter how much or how many times he tried to persuade me to change my mind, and thank God I did, because I still have that time when I belonged to myself to remember now.

We dated all through my college years. I dated other guys too. Dan and I were not exclusive, nor were we engaged to be married. In fact I broke up with him several times.

One time I had battled traffic all the way into Manhattan on a Friday afternoon. It was hot and I was double-parked waiting for a parking space.

Dan yelled at me out his dorm room window, "You're late."

I was furious and pulled away, thinking to myself, *screw this, screw you!*

But, as ever, he called me afterward and begged and pleaded, and

39

took a train out to Bronxville to show up at my house. On most of these occasions, I just wanted him to go away and leave me alone, but he was so persistent.

For my nineteenth birthday, on November 7th, 1966, which was only a few weeks after he had arrived at Medical School, Dan gave me an incredible gift: an extremely large pastel head-and-shoulders portrait of himself. I was so stunned I really didn't have a clue what to say. There's a photo somewhere of me and my friends holding that portrait and laughing our heads off at his temerity. *What an ego!* we kept saying to each other. *Imagine if every guy we dated once or twice gave us one of these. We'd have a whole museum after a while, I guess.* I didn't know what the hell I was supposed to do with it, but I did know that, on top of being doggedly persistent, this new guy, Daniel T. Broderick III, was extremely self-assured, more so than anyone I'd ever met.

In college I took a second major in a new field of study, Early Childhood Education. Because of all my years with young children it was a perfect fit for me and I was sure I'd really love teaching. I could have gone either way, teacher or nurse, because I loved science and medicine too, but I chose the teaching courses eventually.

One of the other guys in Medical School I dated was Peter, a muscular blond athlete who took me skiing at his family's lake house. Tony C, another guy I was seeing, was already in his third year at

40

Seton Med School. Fred M was at Harvard Medical and was studying to be a neurosurgeon, like his dad. I knew that marriage to a doctor would give me a good life. To me, doctors are the closest thing to God we have down here because they save lives and heal people. It would definitely be nice to be married to a successful doctor. But then I also dated a basketball player from Fairfield and a senior from Villanova, because they were nice, tall, big athletic guys and that was my type. It never occurred to me to marry a lawyer. I didn't really like any of the lawyers I had known.

Another time I failed to recognize the danger of being married to such a controlling man was on New Year's Eve, 1967, when Dan went home to visit his family in Pittsburgh. The Finks asked me if I would do them a special favor and babysit for some friends of theirs on short notice. I said, sure. I've always hated the forced gaiety and rampant drunken stupidity of New Year's Eve anyway.

The couple came and drove me to a beautiful house in the woods in Larchmont. I had no idea where I was, but since they were friends of the Finks I knew I had nothing to fear that night. The doorbell rang, and when I answered it, there was Dan. *What? What are you doing here?* was my first reaction.

I didn't realize until many years later that he had been checking up on me to see if I was really babysitting on New Year's Eve. Since I had no reason to lie to anyone, it never occurred to me that anyone would think I might be lying. I just thought he must really love me a lot. But I see now that it wasn't really love; it was possession he was after.

Dan Broderick III at Bronx Zoo

Dan never once wavered from his goal of making me his wife. He would wait, he would do and say whatever was necessary – even agreeing with me when he didn't and doing things I wanted to do when he didn't – until he had me. Nobody ever used the terms 'obsessive-compulsive' or 'stalker' back then, but that is what he was. There's a definite line between devotion and obsession, and Dan had crossed it. He was never going to take no for an answer.

I had this great idea in college to enroll myself in two classes at the same time, as we paid by the semester and not by the credits, so the heavier my credit loads the more money I saved. I ended up having enough credits to graduate after my third year, and all I needed to do was student teaching for the first semester of senior year and then I was done. I could have hung around the beautiful campus for another semester and taken art and mythology classes to pass the time, but I was paying my own way and I wanted to move on.

Over Christmas break in 1968 I stopped by the Superintendent of Education's office in Eastchester just to pick up an application for the following September of 1969. When I got there, there were drop cloths and paint cans everywhere. I saw a nice man in a plaid shirt and told him what I had come for. As it happened he was the superintendent – I had thought he was one of the painters – and after he talked to me for a while, he hired me on the spot to fill a third graded teaching position as soon as Christmas break was over in January.

Well, there went my plans for the next six months until my class graduated in June. I suddenly found myself employed in a full-time teaching position in one of the highest paid school districts in the country, and all before my classmates came back from their Christmas break.

It felt amazing: I was teaching at the Anne Hutchinson School in Eastchester, New York. The school was built on the vacant land directly across the street from 16 Joyce Drive where I had grown up. I already knew all of the families. Some of my students were newborns that I had babysat for way back when. The parents were thrilled to see me, and my Aunt Cay, who still lived on Joyce Road, was teaching there as well.

I was so happy, so happy.

Chapter 5

LET IT RING

In College we all joked that we were right on schedule for our 'Mrs. degrees' and that the next stop would be to get our 'PHTS' – Putting Hubby Through School – diplomas. All of my friends got engaged in senior year and got married right after graduation. I had graduated first, so I would naturally be the first to be headed for wedded bliss too, as it turned out a sort of Pyrrhic victory, if you will, for working so hard.

Now that I was finished with college, I had run out of excuses for not marrying Dan. My entire life plan had been to get married after college, and it was after college, so I said yes. I got a beautiful ring that was handcrafted by an artist in Greenwich Village and my mother was ecstatic. I was marrying a doctor. "The ladies at the Bronxville Women's Club will all be a twitter," she commented with satisfaction.

I was really busy preparing lesson plans and learning how to be a full-time teacher, so I wasn't all that into wedding planning, and I wasn't in a hurry to start, but my mother was. Once she had a wedding – any wedding would have done, I think – she was at full tilt and there was no stopping her. She drove me crazy and was furious that I wasn't more interested in all the arrangements. Not that she would have welcomed my whole-hearted involvement in making those arrangements: my wedding was her show all the way and she had her plans. My dad was from a big Italian family and I'd been dancing at those over-sized elaborate weddings all my life, but this was my mother's first chance – and, as it turned out, her only chance – to plan a big do of her own.

I wanted something entirely different. I wanted a small, sophisticated wedding in Manhattan where Dan and I had spent our time together. I wanted to get married by candlelight at Saint Ignatius, where my parents had been married, and to be taken by horse-drawn carriage to the Oak Room at the Plaza for champagne and dancing.

But my mom was having nothing of that nonsense. She wanted a full sit-down meal at her beach club, *ugh!*, and almost every idea I'd had about my wedding was thrown out completely. Although the wedding we did have looks absolutely beautiful in the photographs, it was nothing like the one I wanted.

I hired a band, my favorite band, that she fired, and when she thought I was too slow picking out the dresses, she went ahead and ordered ones of her own choosing. Her vision for my dress was a joke. It was an Empire-waisted, white-on-white gown with puffed sleeves. At my height I would have looked either like a transvestite or an understudy for the lead in 'Whatever Happened to Baby Jane?' It was a horror show of a dress, so I said no, which didn't go over well. In fact she went so crazy that she tore up all the expensive engraved invitations that she had just spent weeks addressing to all her friends.

It was a nightmare. Dan wanted to elope and get married in Pittsburgh. I was so frazzled I didn't want to get married at all; I just didn't care anymore. And all this was going on while I was teaching from 7am to 4pm every day.

To add to the overall festivities, my mom, as the mother of the bride, had a huge fight with Dan over what he should wear at her wedding. She wanted him in a cutaway morning coat, spats, gloves, etc., to match my father and all the other male guests. He adamantly refused because he had in mind a navy blue pin-stripe, double-breasted suit, with a brightly colored blue and pink flowered tie that he'd found for 99 cents, with a pair of brown wing-tipped shoes to finish off the ensemble. It's one of the few times I have ever known Dan to pull together a look that could have gotten him arrested by the fashion police.

Well, my God, you can only imagine the scenes that ensued. No one had ever stood up to my mother like that, ever. Both Dan and my mother were being ridiculous but he wouldn't budge and she couldn't forgive not getting her way, and I was caught in the middle of their stupid arguments.

By that point, if I wanted anything at my wedding not on my mom's list, I had to pay for it myself, so I ordered my Balenciaga gown from some people I knew from modeling, and my bridesmaids' dresses, and paid for the 1928 Rolls Royce and the driver I wanted to take us from the church to the club. These were the only things I really liked about my wedding. The rest was all her show and she never got over how terribly Dan had treated her. Never.

Dan and I weren't even allowed to invite any of our own friends to our wedding because my mother had so many people she wanted to invite.

We got married during Dan's spring break from Medical School in April, 1969. On our wedding day – or was it my mom's? – when my father walked me down the aisle in that gorgeous weather, in that beautiful church, in my magnificent dress, he pretended to lean over and kiss me on the cheek so that he could actually say in my ear, "Good riddance."

I sobbed throughout the entire ceremony and never heard a word the priest or Dan said. All those months of trying to keep everyone happy had ended with that.

The reception was a blur but again the photos were lovely. I couldn't wait to get out of there.

As the Irish saying goes, "When a thing starts out bad, it can only get worse," and it did.

When I look back, it's really funny that Dan had the nerve to ask anyone to marry him, and that anyone – well, me – was stupid enough to say yes. He had literally nothing to offer. Oh sure, he was going to be a doctor down the road, but when we got married it was my income, my job, my car and my savings that we lived on.

Chapter 6

A HONEYMOON IN PARADISE

The honeymoon was a disaster.

We left directly from the wedding and we were both totally exhausted, and then, on the way to the airport, we realized that we had either lost the gift money or that it had been stolen out of the inside of Dan's jacket pocket, so we were in quite a turmoil by the time we got onto the plane to fly to a private estate on St. Thomas in the British Virgin Islands.

That part sounds fabulous, I know, but Dan got drunk from the champagne during the flight and that night we had to check into a really crummy hotel until we could get out to the estate on the far end of the island the next morning.

As soon as we were in the room, Dan unceremoniously threw me on the bed fully dressed, undid his pants, lifted up my skirt, shoved down my underwear and had sex with me. I suppose that could seem very passionate, masculine and romantic, but it wasn't, it was terrible, especially when he completed this performance by passing out cold on top of me.

I had long known Dan was a drinker, and he knew I hated drunks. He often told me, if I had known him at Notre Dame, I would have hated him because he was drunk all the time there.

I could regale you now with stories of Dan getting drunk while we were dating that would make you wonder where my head was at, but once again I didn't put it together and I didn't see the signs. Maybe I just didn't want to look at them. I knew nothing about alcoholism.

His drinking caused problems on our wedding day and it remained the biggest problem in our marriage until the very end.

Dan acted very weird on the honeymoon. He had brought a suitcase full of books to read for pleasure and he sat by the pool reading them alone all day. He dismissed all the help that came with the house, insisting that he wanted me to cook for him, serve him and clean up afterwards. For some reason it was important to him right from the start that I be the one to do these things, including changing the sheets and doing the laundry. Given that I would have the rest of our lives to do this, I don't know why it had to begin right then, but it did.

He went into town without me one day. Then, when I wanted him to come into town with me, he refused, so I went alone.

It was all a very odd and sad start for us. I heard later that he phoned his brother Larry to bemoan that he had made the worst mistake of his life. That would make two of us thinking that, so, you see, we did have something in common after all.

Chapter 7

THE MEDICAL SCHOOL NEWLYWEDS

When we got back to New York, Dan told me, "This is how we're going to work this. No joint accounts, they are too confusing. You give me all your savings and I'll manage our money."

I had charge accounts, savings accounts and checking accounts of my own. I had paid for my car in cash and kept it fully insured via an annual payment.

I said yes to him. I didn't want to fight with him – I never wanted to fight with him – so I did as he asked.

I viewed marriage as a partnership and Dan viewed it as a matter of possession and ownership, and there is a big difference there. Dan had refused to attend any of the church's prenuptial classes before our wedding, so we never discussed any of this before getting married.

Dan expected his wife to clean, cook, do the laundry, iron his clothes, and make the beds. When he demanded that I iron his underwear, I said, "You've got to be kidding. If you want that done, you're going to have to do it yourself." I mean, it was crazy-making. Who had done all of this for him before our wedding day – his roommate? I was the one who had to get up early to make it to my school in Eastchester by 7am, and came home late, while he got to roll out of bed to walk to class across the street.

I moved into a dorm room with Dan until a married residence became available in September. We had to share a community bathroom with our neighbors. I had to commute from Manhattan to Eastchester every day. My life had taken a nosedive for the worse in a big way.

My mother was still furious about the wedding and was threatening to throw all my things away if I didn't come and get them, even though she had a huge house with a full attic and basement, and no one was using my room anyway, but everything in it had to go, and not to any corner of her house. She said she would not "be used as a free storage place."

That was the first time I lost everything I had ever owned. I managed to save my record collection and some wedding gifts and a few clothes, but not much else. She knew there was no way that I could take anything to that tiny dorm room. She was just getting me back for Dan wearing "that awful suit" to 'her' wedding.

Dan did a couple of things that struck me as bizarre when we were first married, although I knew marriage required some adjustments and I'd never lived with a man before.

One day, I was dressed in a little knit dress with stockings and heels, and I had just come home from a long day and an even longer drive into Manhattan, when he jumped on me from behind, placing one hand around my neck, pinning my arms behind my back with his other hand, and wrapping his legs around mine until we both fell over. I didn't know what he was doing or why, and I couldn't get him off me.

"What are you doing? Please let me up," I protested. I was getting all sweaty from struggling to get free. Finally, I threw my head back at him and he let me go.

Was this normal behavior, the way men usually acted? I still don't think so.

He got a bruise on his cheek where my head hit him, so it looked like I'd given him a black eye. Oh he loved telling that story. It made it look like I'd attacked him, instead of the other way around.

I often think of that incident because it's what Dan always did. He would start something and then always turn it around so that he looked like the innocent party and I looked horrible.

Another time during our first few months of marriage he straddled me in bed, held my arms down, and told me, "You know, I know at least five ways I could kill you and nobody could prove a thing."

This has to be odd behavior for newlyweds, though at the time I thought he was just bragging about all the medicine he had learned. What he was really doing, though, was emphasizing his power and control over me. He was always afraid I would leave him, and I wished I could have left him. I wanted to. I wanted to annul the whole thing right away, but I knew that could never happen in my family. I couldn't leave him and I couldn't go home. All of my things were gone and I had nowhere else to go. Besides, to Catholics, marriage is forever. Dan knew he had me where he wanted me – trapped.

I often wondered if Dan was gay, and I still wonder that today. He had his own demons, having been raised the way he was, and nothing in his life or his view of himself would have allowed him to have come out. I think this could be why he was frequently so angry. It's hard to stay angry at yourself; it's easier to send it outward – like my mother and Dan did – and blame others for where you end up. That's something I've learned all too well over time ... lots and lots of time.

Dan was a dandy, obsessed with clothes and hair and facial products, which I'm guessing is not so typical of straight men even today, and was almost unknown forty years ago. At first I found it kind of attractive as it was so different from what I'd seen in other men. But then he took my savings and went to Barneys and bought this ridiculous-looking striped Nehru suit. No one was wearing anything like that, certainly not in Cornell Medical School, and this was years before the Austin Powers movies. Then he bought the infamous black cape with red silk lining and a top hat – à la Sherlock

Holmes or Count Dracula, take your pick – and that just seemed extreme, even comical, to me. The money they costs was less amusing, though.

His closest friend, Jack, was an openly gay doctor, which was very brave of him for those days. Dan spent every free evening with Jack and visited him for years afterward. Jack had a steady boyfriend but let Dan know that he found him very attractive, though I'm not sure he admired Dan's over-the-top taste in clothing.

Personally, I think everyone owes a huge debt to Oprah Winfrey for opening up difficult topics in a sensitive and non-judgmental manner. It all existed back then but no one dared speak of it. There must have been lots of shame and guilt, as well as a very valid fear of what would happen to you if you were exposed.

Dan's friend Jack was more courageous than most; he was out and open about being gay. That was so uncommon then. Isn't life strange? It was expected of Dan that he would marry, just as it was expected of me, but he was never completely with me. His love making was by rote and in the dark, and he needed to be loaded up on alcohol before he attempted it ... or at least he always was, whether he needed it or not. I had nothing to compare it to, so I had no idea that real love between a man and a woman could be different, not a painful exercise done but never spoken of.

Chapter 8

AND BABY MAKES THREE

Shortly after our honeymoon, I got sick. I am never sick and I hate being sick – I've always had a perfect attendance record at both school and work – so it unnerved me. I was apologizing all the time to Dan for suddenly becoming ill. I didn't want him to think he was married to a sickly female; I knew he'd have hated that.

One night we had dinner at O'Henry's Steakhouse in the Village. When we got home I had terrible heartburn. I'd never had heartburn in my life, in fact I didn't even know that's what it was.

Dan explained it to me, and then added, "You're pregnant."

I was horrified. "*What?* What are you talking about? Why am I pregnant? How did you let this happen? You're a doctor, you're supposed to know about these things. Why didn't you allow me to use birth control, if you wouldn't?"

He just laughed.

I didn't want to be pregnant. I didn't want to add a baby right then because I didn't like anything about being married to him. It felt like doom.

Sex education was not offered at Catholic schools nor in Catholic homes, at least not the one I grew up in. As far as sex went, the approach was that it didn't exist so there was no need to be educated about this imaginary scenario. My mother certainly never addressed it. When I found blood in my underpants one day when I was fourteen, she threw a box of Kotex at me and said, "Use this." That was it. I don't think Dan knew any more about conception and its prevention than I did. My expectations that my doctor husband knew exactly what to do to prevent an unwanted birth were obviously wrong.

So, by the time the rest of my college class graduated in June of 1969, I was working full-time, married and pregnant. I didn't attend our class's graduation. I was working that day. I had to keep working because I was our only source of income. Abortion wasn't yet legal in New York.

When I went to my first OBY/GYN appointment, the doctor discovered that I had *uterus didelphys* (two uteri). He sagely informed me that due to my unusual condition I would never be able to carry a baby to term. At the time that seemed like good news. *Whew! Relief!* So I waited and waited to have a miscarriage that never came.

I worked every day of that pregnancy until the actual day Kim was born on January 29th, 1970. I taught school all day that Friday. I had told my boss that she was due in the spring, because we needed every last paycheck I could swing, and I was afraid they would have insisted I leave if they had known my real due date.

The night she was born, we were hosting a party at our place. I made the food and Dan was supposed to bring the liquor. Dan was taking an elective at a law firm at that time, another foreshadowing of the future that I missed. Anyway, I got home at four and I had cramps, but I didn't think anything of it. I got the food ready for the party and I waited for Dan, who didn't come home. At 8pm the guests started arriving and there was still no Dan, and worse, at least from the guests' standpoint, no liquor either. Fortunately the food was good and the guests were starving Med students, so they stayed anyway.

Dan showed up hours later. He was stumbling and he was drunk. He was accompanied by another drunken lawyer, humorously named Daniel Webster, with an equally drunken woman with smeared red lipstick and a full length fur in tow. I never caught her name. I had been telling one of the Med students that I thought I was in labor but since I was so calm he thought I was joking. I wasn't.

Later, when everyone had left, the pains got really bad. I told Dan that I had to get to the hospital, but he was too drunk to even stand upright. Still, I had to go, so I left with him hanging on my shoulders, totally out of it.

The very first nurse to look between my legs caught the baby on the fly. I still had my clothes on. Dan had passed out in the hall and the doctor hadn't had the time to get there yet, but my baby was in a hurry and she didn't feel like waiting for him.

When the doctor arrived and saw that Kim and I were fine, he went out and woke Dan up to tell him the news.

Dan said, "Let's go get a drink."

So they did.

Because the birth was so easy, I was fine by Monday and could have gone back to teaching, but I had no one to leave the baby with. Dan considered everything to do with children 'women's work' and would have no part of babysitting his own child.

So that was the end of my teaching career at Anne Hutchinson. The very next week I found a doctor and his wife who were looking for someone to watch their five month old child while she went to law school. I brought Kim with me to their house Monday through Friday and babysat other doctors' kids at night. Someone had to make money for us to eat. I returned wedding presents for cash to buy Kim a small portable crib. She had come home to nothing and had started her life in a dresser drawer.

One night while I was breastfeeding her I heard the distinctive sound of car being started up in the street below. *Hmm*, I thought, *that sounds like my car.*

It was indeed my car, being stolen. I had to shrug it off, which I did because I had full coverage insurance. Dan on the other hand turned green when I told him. And when I tried to cheer him up by reminding him we had insurance, he said, "No, you don't."

I said, "Yes, I do, and what's more it's fully paid up until next year."

Lo and behold the financial genius and the head of our household's banking institution, who had insisted that he alone manage our money, had canceled our insurance without telling me. He had gotten a refund which he had carefully re-invested at Barney's department store.

Now I was sick. I had lost my great paying teaching job, which I had loved; my car, which I had also loved and which was also the storage facility for my few remaining possessions, was gone; and I had a new baby to boot ... all within a few short months.

Dan, however, was unfazed by all this. He was still on track; his life hadn't changed all that much. Better yet, Medical School was a draft deferment, so Dan wasn't worried about being sent to Vietnam for as long as he was in Med School. To the Army you weren't a real doctor until you had done a year's internship after Medical School, although thanks to being married and becoming a father, Dan didn't need that particular deferment anymore, which was just as well because he had abruptly decided that he didn't want to be a doctor anyway. Nope, being a lawyer was the thing for him.

It turned out that he had never really wanted to be a doctor. He had only gone to Medical School for the wealth that would follow, but he didn't like the pain and suffering he was witnessing, and he hated touching people. He would have been a pretty scary doctor. Pragmatic

62

about it, and refusing to see Med School as the wasted time and money that it was, he announced that he had heard that someone with an MD/JD could "make a million bucks the first year out."

His mind was already made up. This was what we were going to do.

He graduated in May and we summered at his parents' home in Pittsburgh before he started Law classes in the fall. It was so uncomfortable being there that I actually became nostalgic for our old dorm room. I had no job, no access to money and a baby to feed, and I was living with strangers. Dan was gone all day doing part of an internship, supposedly for money, but I never saw a penny or a paycheck stub. That doesn't mean there wasn't one, I just didn't see it, and during our entire marriage I never once saw one of his paychecks. I didn't know in which banks our account – or accounts – were held, or how much we had or owed. I always handed him my checks uncashed.

Then, after all his work to avoid it, Dan got a draft notice and panicked. If he had to go off to war at that moment he was sure he'd never attend Harvard and never make a million bucks, and besides he hated uniforms.

He made sure that it didn't happen. He had doctor friends of his write letters to the Draft Board saying he had bleeding ulcers and was on medication for them, and it worked. He avoided the draft and, as far as I know, never had ulcers (again).

Chapter 9

LAW SCHOOL DAZE

Shortly after we left Pittsburgh for Cambridge, I realized I was pregnant with the baby who would turn out to be Lee. We had no money, no food, no furniture and no car.

Dan had taken out student loans to pay our rent in a seriously slum basement bootleg apartment. Whatever we were paying, it was overpriced. In fact it would have made a great setting for an endurance reality show. As a bootleg apartment, an illegal add-on cunningly created by putting up plywood walls around a broken boiler in the basement, we had no heat, no windows – since we were underground - – and it's almost pointless to add this, but I will anyway, no hot water. It was winter in Massachusetts and I've never been so cold or so miserable in my life.

The neighbors were really kind. At least they looked kind. It was a solidly Portuguese neighborhood and no one but me spoke English.

Fortunately, Dan managed to sail above our abject situation for the most part. He had bought a motorcycle with his summer earnings and he went off to Harvard Law School every day dressed like he was a man from the best of the Back Bay or Manhattan's Upper East Side. "It's important to make a good first impression," he reminded me, and

I'm certain he did.

I liked looking at him. He was the sole bright spot in that dungeon. He had beautiful, expensive clothes all through Medical and Law School. In an era when T-shirts and sandals were the norm, he wore vests and bow ties and elegantly cut sports jackets. Indeed, he was better dressed than any member of the faculty at Harvard.

I was proud of him and I believed him when he said you had to dress the part to be successful even before you were, and I needed to believe in that success or any kind of future that was less grim than our present. So I lived with it because I wanted him to make it, for us to make it, and when he came home and sequestered himself in the rear room to study, I took in children during the day and went to work at Lord and Taylor on Copley Square on Thursday and Saturday nights.

I had to take the bus everywhere, including the laundromat, because we had no car and I didn't know how to drive Dan's motorcycle. Besides, I was pregnant with Lee at the time.

One night, I was out at the laundromat. Kim was asleep and Dan, who was home, agreed that I could leave her and go alone. As I approached the door of our apartment, I could hear both Kim and Dan screaming from inside. I was panicked and threw open the door.

Dan was hitting Kim. She was ten months old and he was slapping her with both of his hands.

I screamed at him and cried and told him I wanted a divorce, that I was getting a divorce, and that I was leaving him.

He tried to stop me by saying that we were both under a lot of pressure and that Kim had woken up crying and wouldn't stop, and he had been trying to study and he'd lost his temper. I wasn't in a listening mood. My life had turned to utter crap and now he was hurting my baby, and if I wouldn't save myself, I would do it for her and the baby I was carrying.

Kim and I took the midnight Greyhound bus to my parents' place. I hadn't packed anything and it was cold and dark, and I was so tired that I let Kimmy crawl around on that filthy bus floor until her little dress was all black.

That's how we arrived at my mom and dad's house.

My mother let us spend one night there before having my dad drive us back to the bus station and pay our fare home. She told me that she wasn't going to raise my kids, that I was married, and that I had to live with it. She said she'd never liked Dan, but it was too late now – I'd made my choices.

Dan seemed neither surprised nor happy to see us. Nor did he apologize for hitting Kim. But he promised to never do it again, and he didn't. There was nowhere for me to go and whatever happened to me from here on in, there would be no one who wanted to hear about it. I belonged to Dan and he could do what he wanted with me. I'd made my choices. My mother was right.

Things got better on Christmas 1970 when we went to Pittsburgh. Praise be to God, Dan's wonderful grandparents gave us the money to buy an Orange Volkswagen hatchback and it helped so much.

Betty with Kim (2 years) and Lee (1 year) in VW hatchback

Chapter 10

LIFE ON THE GOLD STANDARD

I had always been a happy, friendly, sociable girl who made friends easily, which was good because we moved thirteen times in the next seven years. It's really hard to make or keep friends when you know the day you move in that you'll be moving again soon, but you can at least have friendly acquaintances and I managed that at every place we lived.

I also managed to live with no money, which was less easy but nonetheless necessary. We bought our first bedroom set from a yard sale and we still had it in 1989 when it all ended.

Dan was excruciatingly cheap when it came to anything for the kids or the house. To illustrate this, let me move forward for a minute to 1983 and the 'great socket scandal.'

In 1983, when Dan was making big money for the first time, I made a unilateral financial decision without first consulting him. Yep, without saying a word or asking permission, I just plunged ahead and took a step which I felt would greatly enhance my quality of life in the Coral Reef house.

To fully illustrate the irony of our situation, you need to understand that Dan had me out looking at million dollar houses. In fact he had already bought over a million dollars' worth of property out at Fairbanks Ranch.

So, giddy with this high flying life, I thought I could blithely spend fifty dollars without getting into trouble. In our large tract home at Coral Reef, our master bath off of our bedroom had a long plastic vanity with two sinks. The sink on the left had a medicine cabinet and, below it, an electric socket, as well as a cupboard underneath for towels, hairdryers etc. The sink on the right had nothing. Dan took the left side because he had to get ready for work every morning, and his appearance and products were of the utmost importance to him.

No problem – made sense to me. When we moved in I was just so happy to have a permanent roof for us and the kids, and I rarely used my electric curlers or hairdryer, but when I wanted to use them it was impossible.

I couldn't use Dan's side of the sink, and my side had no outlet, and after a while it bugged me. So one day I called an electrician and had him install a cheap plastic plug on my side. *Hooray for me. Go, Betty*. I was thrilled. *Every woman should have a plug of her own*, I thought.

Dan was furious with me. I had made a decision without his consent. The fifty dollars had come out of my food budget money and I hadn't needed to ask him, and it made him incredibly angry at me.

When Dan was angry he'd seethe, he scowl, he'd slam doors,

break things, kick the dogs, threaten the kids and yell. We were all scared of him when he was like that and the worst part was that you never knew what would set him off or when he would stop. I'd try and keep the kids safe by ensuring they remained as far away from him as possible. Later, when they went to live with him, I wasn't there anymore to keep them safe from his temper and I worried about it all the time – what they might say or do that would set him off.

If I wanted anything like a washer and dryer seven years later, I had to earn the money myself and get it myself, so I did. There was never a time in our marriage that I didn't work to help earn money, while he dumped huge sums on his own without ever discussing it with me. Dan always considered all of our money his alone, to do with as he saw fit.

Everyone now thinks, 'Oh, you were so rich.' If they could only understand how poor we were and for how long. When Dan finally did graduate in 1973 and got a job in San Diego, more than half his paycheck went to paying down those student loans for his education. Yes, he was a lawyer and he wore amazing clothes and drove fancy cars, but at home we were poor. I actually supported this dual lifestyle – our home life and his presentation of himself at the office. I wanted him to be happy and successful so that we could have a happy and successful family life.

When we got to San Diego, I went back to teaching, this time

Fifth Grade, and I worked in a jewelry store nights and weekends, and I was a hostess at a Black Angus Steakhouse. For years.

I'm sorry, I'm jumping ahead of myself here.

Lee was born in July, 1971, and in 1972, when she was one and Kim was two, before the start of Dan's final year of Law School, he took a legal internship in LA. That summer we drove the Volkswagen with our babies across the country from Massachusetts to LA. I hated the cold in Massachusetts, so I was all for the idea of heading west to sunny California.

We lived in a very small dirty apartment while Dan worked in downtown LA at a law firm.

Neither of us liked the congestion of Los Angeles, and one day, while I was with the kids in the park, one of the other young mothers said, "If I could live anywhere, I'd live in San Diego."

I asked her where it was.

She said, "You get on Freeway 5 and go south until you get there."

So that's what we did, running out of gas on the way, something Dan did often, but eventually we made it.

It was a beautiful day and at the time San Diego was clean and uncrowded, and the traffic flowed. Dan looked around and smiled and said, "There's gotta be a law firm here."

When we went back to L.A., he researched Martindale and Hubble and wrote to the three biggest law firms in San Diego. All three were very interested in a Harvard man with an MD from Cornell.

We drove back to San Diego to meet the people at Gray Cary. They wined us and dined us. The wives took me shopping and to lunch on their husbands' orders, like good Stepford wives, and the boys at the firm showed Dan all he could expect if he became one of the masters of the San Diego universe, like them. There would be good times all around.

There was one strange thing, though, that summer. Dan went down to San Diego by himself to meet up again with the guys from Gray Cary. I was home in the little apartment with the girls and nauseous because I was pregnant yet again. I waited till midnight for him to come home, and then I gave up and went to bed. I couldn't sleep. I was worried about him on that long stretch of freeway in the dark. It was 2am, then 3am, then 4am, and by 9am he still wasn't home and he hadn't called. Where was he? Was he even alive?

I called his LA job to see if he had gone straight there but they hadn't seen him. I called my friend Mary Beth around 10am. I was frantic because Dan never carried any ID showing our LA address or phone number. If he was in an accident, they would have had no way to connect him to me and the girls.

He had our only car and all the money, as usual. I didn't know what to do. At around 11am he finally walked in like there was nothing wrong. He told me he had been drunk, which I believed, and that he had pulled off the highway and slept in the car. I asked him why he hadn't at least called me and he said he hadn't wanted to wake me. Ha, very fishy story since he knew what a light sleeper I was and he had to have known I'd be worried sick about him.

He had been with someone I shall call 'Don Manning.' 'Don' and he were very close from that night on. I'm not sure why they had wives and girlfriends; in reality they preferred each other's company over any woman's.

Please don't misunderstand me, or think for one minute that I don't like gay people and don't fully support gay marriage and rights, because I do. Some of the best people I have ever met were gay men and women whom I worked with in the fashion industry, and in fact I've always found gay people to be some of the smartest, funniest, kindest people I've ever known. And they've always been good to me. The problem I had with Dan, and guys like him, is the fraud and dishonesty intrinsic to their denial of who they really are.

No wonder Dan had so much trouble connecting on an intimate level with me. He should just have been honest with himself and me and everyone else, but the way he was brought up he just couldn't face the truth or I guess what he would have seen as the fallout.

74

When it was time to leave LA to drive back over to Harvard, I begged Dan to leave me, the girls and the car out in California and fly back alone to finish his last nine months, emphasizing he could visit us often. But he would not allow that. So back in the hot car we went, trekking across the whole country with two very little girls – one still a baby – and me, his pregnant wife. It was literally nauseating.

Back in Cambridge we got another tiny ghetto apartment and I had trouble, more trouble than usual, enduring this life we'd made together. Abortion had become legal in New York by then and I did not want another baby to be born in these conditions. We couldn't support the two we did have and Dan was never home, and when he was he didn't help at all with our girls. I wanted an abortion; I think I needed one, actually.

Dan and I drove to New York, but he kept telling me he didn't want me to have an abortion, so I changed my mind. He cried and promised that he'd help out more, so we turned around and drove back to Massachusetts, and I continued on with what turned out to be a really terrible third pregnancy which I spent throwing up from one end and bleeding from the other the entire time. The only way I could keep my eye on our two girls, one of them a toddler, was to stay in the bathtub. The girls had no idea that anything was wrong with that. They loved the bathtub.

But Dan had lied to me: he never helped out, not once, not with anything. I bled in the grocery store and at the laundromat while he studied or watched TV and tuned it all out – me, the girls, the pregnancy. We were flat broke and we didn't go out once that year, not to a single dinner or a movie. I hadn't bought a pair of shoes or even one piece of clothing since the day we had gotten married. I made my own maternity clothes and when our third child was born Dan was away skiing with friends.

I was bleeding badly after falling on the ice when I had come out of the grocery store, and I had to leave the girls with a neighbor I barely knew and call the police to take to me to the hospital because I didn't have cab money. There was a snowstorm that night, too, just to cap it all off.

The baby was born breech, like both of the girls had been, and he was a little boy, our first son. He was seven pounds and fair and beautiful, and he lived for a day, but they only let me see him after he was dead. This was in the February of 1973. We never named him or buried him, so I still don't know where he is.

Dan said we couldn't afford to bury him and he wasn't sorry about the baby. In fact he was angry at me for ruining the first ski trip he had been able to take for years and continued to go on about it for days.

That was the first time I tried to kill myself.

76

Dan was so cold and detached, and I felt totally trapped with him and cut off from my family. My family had never liked him and he hated them and was openly rude to them whenever he saw them. I had small children and our financial net worth as a couple was minus hundreds of thousands of dollars in student loans that I was somehow half liable for if we split up. In fact I was still paying my half of his monthly student loan payments in 1989.

I just wanted to escape from it all and die. I was twenty-three and I couldn't face decades more of this existence. I told myself that our girls were so young that they wouldn't even miss or remember me, and I knew that my family would raise them and give them a better life than I could ever offer them.

I swallowed every pill I could find in our medicine cabinet. Sadly, they were not good enough to work and I woke up when Dan aroused me. He said things would be better in California and that I only needed to hold on for a few more months. He never said anything about us as a couple or about our lost baby. Still, I agreed with some of what he was saying and began to hope again for better times. That's a hard thing to kill in people, hope, especially when you are young.

I didn't really want to die. I just wanted different, better. Maybe California was the answer. It would be warm there, the sun would shine all the time, and Dan would have a paying job.

So I held on.

Chapter 11

GO WEST, YOUNG FAMILY

In May 1975 we drove back across the country again. We had our girls but no furniture, no belongings and no friends or family waiting to meet us when we got there.

When we arrived in San Diego, Dan left us in real hell-hole of a motel and went off to find us a place to live. He was gone all day and he hadn't even been apartment hunting. He'd been with Don Manning. He was drunk and he was now driving a brand new MG that he had just bought on credit. It had been a long day, he told me, so there hadn't been time to look for a place for us to live yet.

Don was a problem in our marriage from the day we arrived in San Diego. He took Dan 'under his wing' at the law firm where there was a lot of cheating and after-hours playing offside. Don was into drinking and carousing with the secretaries after work, and when Dan first got there he was incredulous when he described what was happening, although, as he became more involved, he stopped telling me about what was going on there.

From the first, Dan was a great lawyer, or a great professional liar, take your pick. He was very good at lying to your face and he could convince anyone of anything, even though they knew otherwise.

He was also extremely boyish-looking and was always impeccably dressed, with a rose in his lapel. San Diego hadn't ever seen anything like him.

His plan was to stay at the firm for five years and then, just before making partner, he would leave and go out on his own. He said it would be much harder to leave after making partner, but Dan believed you could never get rich working for someone else. So for the next five years everything we did was with the firm. It was like a cult.

All I ever wanted to be was a good mom to a brood of chicks. Through all the years of constant upheaval and moves, Kim and Lee were adorable. I absolutely adore my children, from the first moment of the day to the last, and still do. They were my priority and I wanted so badly for them to have a happy childhood. I never remembered being happy or playing with my mom. She always seemed very aloof and distant. I didn't want to be that way and I made a real effort to hug and hold and play with my kids on the floor from their very first days. Kids are mostly oblivious to the problems in the world around them. They need to be fed, changed, bathed and cuddled. I kept mine well fed, clean, safe, warm and happy as best I could in bad circumstances. Kim and Lee were all my happiness and my life because Dan was so busy building his career and had very little time for the three of us.

After the baby died in 1973, I had a few months there without a newborn and without being pregnant. It was just me and my girls. When we arrived in California, we rented a little apartment at The Plum Tree and I got a half-day teaching job at Saint Columbia's Catholic Church in Serra Mesa, within walking distance of our home. I was only gone during the girls' afternoon nap time and I was happy to be back in the profession I loved.

Then disaster! Before school started in September I began to feel queasy. *Oh no, not again.* Dan would never even discuss using birth control and the pill made me feel as nauseated as my pregnancies did. The I.U.D. didn't work because of my two uteruses and Dan said diaphragms were "disgusting" to him and condoms "out of the question," so I was constantly pregnant. I wanted a large family, yes, but I had envisioned a home and an involved husband and father in that dream. The years of constant moving had really taken a toll on me, and I felt isolated and lonely because Dan was never home and we hadn't stayed anywhere long enough to become a part of any community. Dan's community was his school and work, and those things had remained consistent for him in spite of where we lived.

I was still badly traumatized by the death of our firstborn son only a few months before and I was not ready to be sick again for another nine months, and that's what my pregnancies always brought with them. We had just arrived in California and I had gotten a nice job. Another pregnancy would have ruined everything. Abortion was legal and easy in California by that September of 1973. I know when I'm pregnant right away and I told myself there was no fetus, no baby, just a tiny speck.

I made an appointment and went and did it.

But before the year was over, I had become pregnant again. That ended in a miscarriage and I was able to teach school for both semesters.

Chapter 12

A very Merry Christmas.
And a Happy New Year,
I hope it's a good one without any fear.

John Lennon

We had to move from the Plum Tree apartments when there was a short-out at the pool right outside our door, and we found a small rental on Biddle Court, in Claremont, which became our very first little house. For the first time the girls had a backyard and I had saved enough from my tips at Black Angus to buy a washer and dryer finally. From my standpoint, life was getting better. Indeed, it was pretty great.

That December we had a little tree and I spent my whole teaching paycheck from September through October buying presents for our families back east. Meanwhile, Dan bought himself a present with one of his paychecks – an 'Instant On' color TV. Dan had always loved watching TV.

One evening we got a sitter and went out Christmas shopping for the last two gifts we needed before I could send them all off to his family in Pittsburgh. While we were gone, the new TV set somehow shorted and set the curtains in the living room on fire and the house burnt down. At that moment all that was important to me was that my little girls were okay. They were, so thank God.

All that was left was a charred, stinking mess and, Merry Christmas, we had to move again. On the upside, there wasn't much packing to do for our latest move.

Betty with Kim and Lee

We relocated to a temporary apartment while the house was being rebuilt. That took a year. When we moved back into the house, the elderly owners were so pleased with the brand new house that they had gotten as a result of the fire that they wanted us out immediately so they could sell the place. So the next Christmas was a sad little one too, since we had to move once more to another temporary apartment where we didn't know anyone, although, as the old cliché goes, 'every cloud has a silver lining.' As horrible as that fire and the subsequent moves were, they turned out in the end to be a real blessing for us, since by that time Dan was a lawyer in the biggest and most powerful law firm in town and I got to witness for the first time the formidable power of lawyers in action.

We had renters' insurance, and with Dan calling them they couldn't do enough for us. Prior to the fire we had purchased some basic furniture on in-store credit and it had all burned too, and they bent over backwards to pay us for every itsy-bitsy worthless item we owned. Also, because Dan had a regular job, we could get loans. But Dan didn't use any of our insurance money to pay off the in-store credit. Years later we were still paying for it even though it was long in ashes.

Dan's great friend Don was very helpful to us during that time. He bullied the insurance company, saying that the "firm was a powerful legal force to reckon with" – I can't argue with him there – and went so above and beyond in his assistance to us that he was the one who actually found us a house to buy in his neighborhood.

With some extremely fancy and elaborate financing, Dan

parlayed our insurance settlement into a partial down payment on the house on Coral Reef. He then finagled a second mortgage from the seller to make the rest of the down payment on the first mortgage, with the proviso that a balloon payment was to be made in five years back to the original seller on the second mortgage. Pretty creative.

The result of all this wonder-working financial genius, though, was that we now had huge debts on top of the student loans, and nothing we had was paid for. It was all financed to the hilt and we could barely get by month by month.

We moved to Coral Reef in December of 1975, December having become our annual move month by this time.

I was very pregnant with Danny and we had no furniture and no food, but we did have our first house. It turns out it was our only house, but that story comes much later.

Chapter 13

CORAL REEF: THE BEGINNING OF THE END

A house is made of bricks and beams.
A home is built with love and dreams.

It was a California tract house with very cheap construction – slab and stucco and dry wall, low cost aluminum siding and doors and windows, and with no curb appeal. From the street it looked like a three-car garage with an entry to the left. It was nothing like the houses either of us had been raised in back east.

But that was okay because it was ours, sort of, and there were lots of pluses to it too: It was super-convenient to the I5 freeway and Dan's job; it was close to Don; it had a big backyard for the children; and it afforded us five bedrooms and two family rooms, one with a fireplace.

We loved it, and from my point of view it had tons of potential.

Daniel T. Broderick IV, aka 'Danfourth,' was born only weeks after we moved in. The firm gave him lots of welcome-to-the-world presents, including little pants with 'Junior Partner' printed on the back. Dan was thrilled, too. Danny's arrival meant that we could finally have sex again. From my side I thought that now he had his son and his career and his house, surely he would have more interest in our family.

Coral Reef, 1977 – Dan kept this family photo in his office

However Dan was way too busy to spend any time with me and the children. I loved him and I admired him, and I did respect how hard he worked, but he brought work home every night and worked on weekends as well, and he logged three times the hours that any of the other young associates did. I was very proud of him and his success, but I paid the price for all those hours he was away from his home and his little family.

He was working for us, though. That's what he always told me.

As for our mountain of debts, long before the rest of the country learned to live (and then fall) on credit, our family were pioneers in the movement. Dan's brother Larry helped show us the way. Larry was into finance and he was making a lot of money. He was younger than Dan but his family already had a nicer house, and they had great cars and trips, and even indoor furniture. Larry hadn't spent all those years in Graduate School, like Dan, who hadn't earned any money for the seven years he spent in Grad School and who had amassed a tremendous debt we had to pay off. Dan finally had a job but we were still seriously 'cash poor,' so Larry taught Dan about leveraging things.

I was there when he said, "Say you have a hundred dollars. Instead of spending that money, you can get credit and spend ten times what you have. Then you use your hundred dollars in cash to make the minimum monthly payments on the thousand dollars' worth of stuff you bought."

This ideology sounded like a solid financial plan to Dan, so that's how he managed our money. Nothing was ever paid for and everything was leveraged and financed to the maximum. The house, the cars, and every piece of furniture and clothing, and even our groceries, were handled this way, all through the magic of credit cards.

Betty with Lee, Kim and Danny

I was uncomfortable with living way beyond our means but I had no say in finances. Money, and the handling of it, was 'men's work,' and I was only responsible for 'women's work,' which, as it always has throughout time, entailed taking care of the children and the house, preparing meals, doing laundry, and over time in our case, entertaining his legal friends and accompanying him to functions while looking adoring.

That wasn't hard for me. I really was a supportive wife and I wanted him to be successful and happy, and I worked hard all the time to please him. More than anything in the world I wanted Dan to be happy, to be happy with me. I always thought that if he was happy, we'd all be happy. He was the king in our household and his moods affected everyone, a kind of trickle-down home emotional economics, if you will. If he was happy there was less tension, and so I made the his drinks and had them ready for him when he walked through the door. It sounds ridiculous and archaic but I truly believed this was what I was supposed to be doing, what I needed to be doing to make everything right for all of us. I knew how hard he worked and I wanted him to relax when he got home and be glad he was there. He liked pina coladas and I put lots of liquor in them to mellow him out at night. He hated to see any vestiges of the children around the house and would fly into a rage if he saw toys or playpens, or, worst of all a high chair, in *his* house.

When Dan was not at home the children and I were relaxed and happy, but come 4pm I started getting tense, worrying about how everything looked before he came home. It was always like that in our

91

marriage.

Dan was a compulsive neat freak and I found that a very attractive trait at first. Later, when we had more children, I started to see it as a sickness and a way to frighten me and control every aspect of our home life. His rages scared me, just as my mother's had when I'd been a child. He and she both would yell and scream, and rant and rave, and smash things when they were angry.

Like our home life, the way Dan handled finances was very controlling, and therefore abusive, but that's the way he insisted it be from Day 1 of our marriage. I was on a very tight budget. He gave me twenty-five dollars a week for the first several years we were married and I had to buy all the groceries out of that. It went to thirty-five, and then fifty later on, so no wonder I worked all the time, and anyway I wanted to work and make my own money. I hated the way he controlled me with *his* money.

Before I married him, having my own money gave me a lot of freedom. I earned it and I could spend it as I wished. Dan always considered everything he bought as his: it was *his* house, *his* car – never *ours* – and he controlled all of it. He was in charge of our lives and made all the decisions. I never thought it was abusive, I just thought he was a very high-strung, difficult man who was under enormous pressure all the time, some of it self-imposed. It was my job to keep him from exploding. Later on, when I had a checking account and charge cards, my every expenditure had to pass his scrutiny.

One day in 1975 I went shopping with my next door neighbor on Biddle Court. Her husband was a doctor, so we had that in common, as well as having two toddlers. She had gone to Smith and I was really happy to have her as a neighbor and potential new friend.

I'll never forget that shopping trip. I bought a thirty-five dollar dress. It was colorful, comfortable and washable, but I was so scared because I was sure I would get in trouble for buying it without asking him first. That's how we lived. The experts later said that I was in an abusive relationship the whole time because I had no freedom and no choices about anything. Even his refusal to discuss birth control methods was abusive. I was kept as the not-so-modern version of barefoot and pregnant, with no way to escape his unshakeable dictates and control.

Mind you, I was not a feminist. I wanted to be a wife and mother. I did not spend my marriage trying to wrest power and control away from him. We modeled our marriage on his parents' marriage. That's how his father was. He controlled all the money in the family and his wife had a household budget; the rest of the finances were none of her business. Like me, she never knew if they were rich or poor, and didn't have a single idea of what their debts and/or investments were. She just had to manage the household within the prescribed budget he allowed her.

93

I went along with everything Dan wanted because I wanted a happy home and family life more than I wanted anything else. No matter what has been said about me, what I've always felt is that the things that matter most aren't *things* at all.

Dan never consulted me or informed me of major purchases he made, even when he came home with a ridiculously flashy car he bought in the airport while he was on a business trip. It was a fiberglass 'replicar,' built on a Ford Pinto chassis. It was not a fun car to drive. It rattled a lot and had no power steering. Actually, it was a piece of junk underneath but on the outside it looked good to Dan, and he said he felt like the 'Fresh Prince of Bel Air' in it. It attracted attention and Dan always craved that.

I used to tease him that his gravestone was going to read, "Here Lies Dan Broderick who always got maximum FLASH for minimum CASH." I always thought that was funny because it was totally true.

Before, during and after Linda I was a lonely woman in my marriage to Dan. I loved my kids but I was always the only grown-up in that house. Dan was rarely home, and when he was, he wasn't talking much, which is why, although I didn't realize it until many years later, I loved having a*u pair* girls in my home six months at a time. They came from several different countries – England, Sweden, Germany and France – and each one of them was truly wonderful.

94

It was fun for me to have someone to talk to, and, yes, to have an extra set of hands to help with the children, of course, but more important than that was the safety. Dan would never be violent or act crazy if anyone was there to witness it. He was very concerned with his image and he couldn't afford for anyone to witness his violent episodes.

He even hid a lot of them from me. I wasn't there when he put his fist through the wall in Los Angeles. I wasn't there when he took the door off the hinges and the frame out of the wall at Coral Reef. I wasn't there when he went next door to borrow a sledge hammer to smash our lawnmower to bits.

He scared me when he acted like an insane maniac. I'd cry and get upset, and he'd get mad at me for crying and tell me, "Next time it will be you if you don't shut up."

The kids witnessed a lot of his rages. When he had sole custody, I was afraid for them. Dan never had live-in help at his house for just this reason. He couldn't risk anyone seeing him lose control like that. The kids told me about his rages when something on his new yacht didn't work. Apparently he screamed and yelled and smashed a bunch of things, before throwing them overboard. I was relieved that I hadn't been there to see that. It's interesting to me that he sort of forgot all this when reciting *ad nauseam* how I threw a ketchup bottle at him once.

95

The children saw quite a bit of these adult tantrums but we never spoke about it. I don't know exactly what, if anything, they remember. It was embarrassing to have such a violent, temperamental husband and I didn't want the *au pairs* to know. They had weekends off, and when they'd come back on Monday and see the damage, I brushed it off and changed the subject. I was ashamed of the truth and didn't want them to tell anyone. Everyone thought we were such a nice family.

Several years later, one of the *au pairs*, Catherine, who I thought I had hid it from, came to testify about what she had seen and heard while she lived with us. It turns out she had been horrified by the way Dan treated me even back then. My lawyer, Jack Earley, did not call her as a witness. Nor did he call Brian Burchell, who, like Catherine, had firsthand knowledge and had lived at my house and seen it up close and personal. Both had wanted to testify and help me, and neither was ever heard from.

Lawyers are a strange bunch, at least the ones Dan hung with at Gray Cary, where they all made a lot of money, they all had big houses and nice cars, and took lots of trips, and partied all the time. Since we didn't know anyone else when we moved to San Diego, they were the only people we met. They really were a lot of fun to be around and were pretty entertaining when they were drunk. And, from the first,

Dan fit right in.

Now, in no way am I suggesting that all lawyers are like this. I have lots of friends and relatives who are very successful and have all the stuff – houses, cars, etc. – and still go home to their families at night. These are the sober ones.

Dan convinced me that all the firm's four-hour lunches and after-hours office parties were an essential part of building his career. I accepted that as truth to a certain extent. Don arranged all these Saturday morning soccer games, and after the games they all went to the 'World Famous,' which is an old-established place in Pacific Beach, where they had big brunches washed down by lots and lots of drinks. Dan enjoyed himself at these gatherings and I liked that he participated because it meant that he took a break from working all the time.

I did have some other leisure ideas for him that I tried to interest him in, such as running, golf or tennis. I thought he could use these to relieve stress and that I could have joined him, at least part of the time. He wasn't biting, though.

I was glad that he liked the soccer games on Saturday, or I was until I heard that the secretaries were welcomed at the after-game card parties, but the wives weren't. After that I didn't like the games at all. Don was always going on about the lame things wives did and I was starting to hate him for his attitude to my kind.

Saint Patrick's Day was always huge in New York City, at least in the Sixties. Dan had never really been a part of anything like that before. All the Catholic college kids, and anyone else who felt Irish on that day, went crazy drinking and partying after the big Saint Patrick's Day parade down 5th Avenue. We were too poor while we were in Boston to go out to celebrate Saint Patrick's Day, but when we got to San Diego we went out looking for the action on that day ... and found none. We were very disappointed, and so the next year I had a party at the house with an old-fashioned corn beef and cabbage dinner, and green beer and wines, with Irish music playing. I even made green scrambled eggs for breakfast and put shamrock toilet paper in the bathroom.

I know a lot of Irish songs, since I taught school with Irish nuns at Saint Columbia's School, and I even had a Kazoo band with my Fifth Grade class, and we marched around the school playing 'McNamara's Band' and 'When Irish Eyes are Smiling.' We had so much fun. Saint Patrick's Day has always been a big deal for me since I'm half-Irish and from New York.

When we moved to Coral Reef I changed parishes to go to Saint Brigid's in Pacific Beach. The girls were small then and Danny was a newborn. Saint Brigid's had a small group of guys who sang and played guitars at Mass, and that's where I met Michael Reidy.

I insisted that Dan accompany me to one of the Irish dinners the church gave that year. Dan had adamantly refused to attend Mass with me and had never agreed to have our children baptized into the church – so much for having married a Catholic. Dan told me after we were married that he didn't even believe in God. I ignored him and attended church whenever I was able. I had to take all the kids with me because he had to work or to sleep, and moreover he was not going to be "my babysitter."

Back to Saint Brigid's, at that Irish dance I introduced Dan to Mike Reidy. Mike, who was one hundred percent Irish, had always wished he could have gone to Notre Dame, and there was Dan who actually had attended, and he and Dan hit it off and became friends. I even hired Mike to sing at our next Saint Patrick's party.

Mike was not a lawyer, he was just a great guy, and I was glad of their friendship since I liked Mike too and I was hoping to get Dan out from under the ever-annoying Don's pervasive influence. I was already looking forward to the day that Dan left Gray, Cary and went out on his own.

Chapter 14

A WOMAN OF CONVICTION

I am a woman of conviction. Well, actually, now I am a woman of multiple convictions ... but that didn't come until much later.

When Dan joined the firm, one of the couples who had befriended us lived close by and had two little boys. They had invited Dan and me and our girls over to their house several times. When we were there, Dan talked shop to the husband and drank. We wives and kids had fun preparing the food and indulging in 'girl talk,' and that's how it always was at the firm.

Years later, before we had any troubles of our own martially-speaking, that same husband cheated on his wife and she was devastated. I felt so sorry for her. I couldn't imagine surviving that: the rejection, the shame, the fear, the guilt at your own inadequacy, and the heartbreak.

That's the worst of it, the endless heartbreak.

Well, later on, that same husband married his secretary and the reception was on a Saturday night at the Bahia Resort on the bay, right down the hill from our house.

For once I really stood up to Dan and said I wouldn't go, which was no easy matter as he could be both intimidating and persuasive when he wanted something, but I felt very strongly about this.

Dan had already left the firm by then, so it was even more important to him to go to their wedding since it was a 'firm event,' and he very much still wanted to be part of their herd.

I adamantly refused to go. I told him that I could never be that

101

fake and phony, and I couldn't raise a glass to their health and happiness after what he had done to my friend and their family.

Dan would not take no for an answer. He really wanted me to go.

I told him to go by himself if he wanted to attend so badly but that I was not going. I couldn't compromise myself and my values just to go along with the firm crowd.

He was furious but I felt really proud of myself for finally not giving in to his power to control me. It takes a lot of guts to stand up to your abuser, but oh it feels so good when you do.

Years later, very few of the wives had the conviction not to attend Dan and Linda's wedding out of loyalty to me. They were all hanging onto their own marriages for dear life and trying to please their own husbands. It didn't and doesn't work. The same fate befell every one of them eventually, and it was only then, after it happened to them, that they finally understood how painful feeling ostracized and betrayed by your close friends was.

I've noticed that women rarely stick together like men do. I think it's because they don't feel in control of their own lives. Women who are dependent on men have to defer to them rather than believing in and developing their own power.

Chapter 15

FLYING SOLO

Hold your horses. I know you're probably getting bored with all these little details. You want me to hurry up and get to the good parts, the parts you see in the movies about my life, the ones the District Attorney helped make. But stay with me, be patient, because all the little threads and stories are essential to the tapestry of my life, of who I am and how our marriage worked.

If all you want is that story, it's been written. This is my story and I want you to know me. I'm so hoping that you want to, so please stay with me, okay? Throw this book away or take a break if you must, but I have to lay the foundation for what came later.

That's what the D.A. had no knowledge of or interest in whatsoever. She didn't want to know the truth of what happened, because the truth might have helped me. Concerning herself as to what truly happened was not something she cared about, that wasn't her job. I understand that. Winning is everything.

In the world of San Diego legal circles my own experience lends itself to the belief that winning is all, that truth and justice are nothing; that in San Diego it was the 'just-us' system at work.

The time was drawing close for Dan to enact his original plan to leave Gray, Cary and go out on his own at the five year mark. This was a giant move for us. It would, and did, take guts, courage and faith to walk away from the only regular paycheck he had ever had.

All our so-called possessions were leveraged to the max. We had large debts that had to be paid toward every month and the balloon payment was coming due on our house's second mortgage. We didn't have a penny saved toward that and, to top it all, it was 1978 and I was pregnant again.

In the three years between Rhett and Danny I had another miscarriage and a second abortion, but despite this I wanted another baby. I wanted Danny, my Danfourth, to have a brother to grow up with. I had decided that if this baby was a girl, I would have another child because I really believed Danny needed a brother.

When it turned out that Rhett was a boy, a totally gorgeous one to boot, I had my tubes tied. During this period of our lives I had begun slowly to come into my own power. Maybe I was finally growing up, or maybe, after so many years with my mother's and then Dan's hand on the back of my neck, I'd just passed beyond people being able to control me totally. After that, for the first time in a decade, I was not always sick and pregnant. I was feeling and looking great. The tubal ligation was in self-defense. I was so tired of being pregnant all the time. I do understand that abortion is not an acceptable form of birth control, and maybe I had no right to do it, but Dan would not use, or allow me to use, contraceptives. My abortions destroyed me as well as the baby, and my tubal ligation ended the mental as well as physical anguish of my seemingly non-stop pregnancies once and for all.

Rhett's homecoming to Coral Reef

By that time it was quite evident that Dan would never be the involved father or husband of my dreams. I was always a single parent and I was always going to be one. Four kids were plenty for me to handle on my own.

Catholic hospitals and doctors wouldn't do tubal ligations back then. I don't know if they do them now. To get mine I had to switch to a different doctor and hospital, and since my husband was a medical malpractice attorney, it was nearly impossible to find any doctor who would take me as their patient.

Dan used to joke, "Bets, if anything ever happens to me, like a car accident or something, get me on a life flight far away from San Diego. After all I've done to these doctors, they'd love to have me under their knives for a change."

So there we were, ready to take the leap. Dan was frightened and he started second guessing himself and his original five year plan. For my part I very much wanted him to get away from Gray, Cary, so I encouraged him to set up on his own. I told him that I didn't care if we lost the house and had to go back to apartment living. I said it would be worth it in the long run. Yes, it would be scary, but together we could do it.

It was scary and we did do it.

Dan got a five hundred thousand dollar line of credit at the bank to get started. He originally planned to lease a cheap office space on the wrong side of Broadway in downtown San Diego and rent a cheap metal desk and filing cabinet until he made money. I told him it didn't work like that. I said that, "Success begets success. You have to fake it till you make it. You have to look like you're a top lawyer who really knows what he's doing to inspire and instill confidence in your clients. Dan, you have to trust in your own prowess and capabilities, or why should anyone else?"

Of course all my Vince Lombardi cheering didn't change the bottom line that by doing this we were going to go even further into debt. I ignored my own worries, shored up Dan's confidence, and got myself a decorator's license so we could at least buy wholesale.

We went to L.A. where we ordered really beautiful dark oak furniture: a credenza and filing cabinets, and client chairs. We got expensive brass accessories and one hundred percent pure wool plaid fabric on the chairs. I ordered wide whale corduroy for the nail head sofa, and dark blue carpet. Dan leased corner office space in a brand new building in downtown San Diego. His corner was cut on the diagonal so he had a panoramic view of San Diego Bay and the Coronado Bridge. It was gorgeous. We got silk plants and trees and flowers, and when it was done it was positively sumptuous and the envy of every other lawyer in town. No problem that nothing was paid for and that he had no clients, since nobody else knew that except me, and my plan worked too.

Dan didn't want to have an opening party in his office because he was still Mr. Neat Freak and he was terrified that someone would smoke or leave drinks on his new furniture. This little tidbit becomes important later, so bear with me.

That's how it began. He was launched on a wing and a prayer, and best of all from my standpoint, he was away from Don, at least for the moment.

I've always loved interesting, stimulating conversation and I was eager to hear about Dan's various cases, just as I had been fascinated by listening to his stories about classes at Medical and, later, Law School.

Dan used to tell me all about the various outrageous antics at the law firm: How they bullied this client or cajoled that one, and who they extorted to make things go their way. Duh, winning!

Dan thought it was funny and he told me about the "nasty grams" he carefully worded to people to intimidate and scare them. He'd tell me about all the mean dirty tricks he'd use to hurt and humiliate people, doctors mostly, and he'd laugh about it. He considered himself the cleverest of them all and master of his domain, the arena of law. He was so horrible to a doctor he had on the stand once that the man broke down and began to cry. Dan was elated by this success.

Dan always went for punitive damages in the court room. "Punies," as he called them, were what really hurt. They were not covered by malpractice insurance and there was no cap on how much you could get. These damages came out of the doctors' own pockets.

For Dan, the more "punies" he could get the better, but it was more than that for him.

Dan seemed to like to, or maybe needed to, inflict humiliation and suffering. It wasn't good enough just to have the insurance companies pay out millions; he wanted to personally hurt the doctors. I've always loved doctors, and as far as I'm concerned it's very rare, if ever, that a doctor has purposely harmed someone. Actually except for Dr. Mengele in Germany, no one comes to mind. It's true that bad things do happen but I don't believe there is malicious intent involved in them.

Dan was good with juries. He could paint these elaborate mental images of pain and suffering, and he could turn a hangnail into a lifelong disability and the cause of an agonizing lifetime of pain and suffering. Basically what I think is that courtrooms are all theater and drama. Dan had the acting skills and the looks for his role, so he won there. That's all it boils down to.

Another aspect of Dan's success was who he knew in the legal community. To promote himself and his practice, he became heavily involved in the Bar Association and its politics. It was a natural for him, since he had always loved anything associated with the word 'bar' in it.

Other lawyers were frankly in awe of Dan's dual Harvard Law and Cornell Medical degrees. He dressed flamboyantly and always stood out in any crowd he was in. He began teaching continuing education classes through the Bar Association to other lawyers on Saturdays. He did this as a 'favor' to the judges and his influence didn't end there. He was also on a Bar Association committee that selected and endorsed certain judges for re-election and re-appointment. The judges loved Dan and he did as many favors for them as he could. One judge's mother tripped and fell on a sidewalk. Dan sued the city and got her a lot of money and refused his fee, knowing he would be amply paid back in other ways.

He shared all of these moving little stories with me as they occurred. It was how things went in San Diego, and elsewhere too, I guess. *You do for me and I'll do for you, quid pro quo,* moves the world, doesn't it?

Dan may have networked on the grand scale but he worked alone. He had hired a secretary, Sharon, who was his typist and who transcribed what he dictated, but she wasn't an employee in that sense. Sharon was a private contractor, which meant that Dan just paid her by the hour, without a salary or benefits. Dan was always cheap unless it was for show, and then the sky was the limit.

In private practice Dan still worked very long and arduous hours, and he did it seven days a week, the difference being that now he was working for himself. At home I helped him with ideas and listened while he practiced his arguments. At that time we were really happy

110

and really together as a couple. I had accepted him for who he was and how he was, and I felt he had done the same with me. He certainly seemed to be proud of me and that meant more than anything. I guess it *was* everything to me, sad to say. I always made a good showing for him. I entertained all his friends and clients regularly, and my New York background and French cooking school lessons came in very handy. At that time the see-saw was balanced very nicely. I loved cooking and entertaining, and I think I did it pretty well. I tried hard and that was my contribution to his success, and I took pride in it. I think he did too.

We started to become well known as a couple. The kids were going to school and I became heavily involved with everything to do with that and the soccer teams and Brownies and Cub Scouts and at church. I met and befriended a lot of people and raised our profile in the suburbs.

Dan was well known downtown all on his own. His practice was going extremely well and early on he became able to pick and choose only the biggest cases that came his way. He referred out all the lesser ones and a lot of lawyers got rich on those referrals.

Dan used to tell me how funny it was that, "every time a guy gets a big settlement, the first thing he does is go out and buy a red sports car, always red. And then he dances with his wife. Never fails." He always thought that was hilarious right up until he went out and did

111

the same thing himself.

Dan's cases took two to three years from the day they walked into his office until the day they got the check. In his specialty nobody paid up front; it was all on contingency. So in 1978 through 1980 we lived on the original line of credit until the cases began paying off, and we re-financed the house on Coral Reef with a home improvement loan that we used to pay off the balloon payment we owed on the second mortgage – creative financing at its finest.

Even though Dan presented himself as a successful attorney, the truth was that we were still deeply in debt and barely treading water. I still have no idea of how much of the line of credit we used and I didn't know the amount or the terms of the home improvement loan that he got from the bank. The bank was investing in his potential to repay the loans based on his MD/JD degrees. Everyone was always impressed with Dan Broderick, no one more so than himself.

It was a long dry season and we hoed our row hard to plant the seeds of his success. By late 1981 or 1982 the cases started coming in and settling regularly. Dan had made a name for himself, and so more and more defendants wanted to settle rather than face him in trial. That was fast and easy money for Dan, the first of its kind. We could finally relax and get some breathing space, and to celebrate I wanted to buy a sofa. We never had anywhere to sit at night. He had a leather recliner that he used to watch TV in but we needed a sofa.

The answer was, "Nope, Bets, no we don't."

We had these neighbors, the 'Johnsons,' on both sides of our house on Coral Reef. The Johnsons on one side were Catholic and had ten kids, and were very nice, as were all ten of their children. Their kids were older than ours as they were older than Dan and I, and they wanted to encourage us to attend a marriage encounter, that's a Catholic weekend arranged by the church to help make your marriage stronger. They offered to watch our children so that we could go. Dan, naturally, was reluctant but finally agreed to go because I wanted to so much. I thought we needed a weekend away to ourselves, free from the demands of his job and the kids.

Dan learned many things in Law School, primary among these the rule 'deny, deny, deny,' and while you are doing that make sure you never put anything in writing because it can, and most probably will, be used against you later. Sadly for Dan, the entire marriage encounter weekend was based on writing things in books and then switching with each other to read them later. I kept and referred to these books many times over. I know parts of them by heart. I still have them here with me in prison, both because they were a part of the trials and because they are a reality check for me. I had to refer to them to see if I made it all up in my head.

It was sometime in 1979 when we went. Dan was already in his own practice and we had all four children and I had already tied my tubes. All the really hard years of having babies and building a practice were behind us, but I longed for a more intimate relationship with him.

When I wrote of my loneliness and my unhappiness at his lack of time with me and the children, he seemed to understand. He wrote in his book, "Please give me more time. We have both sacrificed, you more than me, to get where we are." He went on to write about the financial goal he had set for himself – a million dollars a year – and

114

how he would only have the time to be a good son, grandson, husband and father (yes, in that order), after he reached his goal. He begged me to be patient and to give him more time, so I did.

By 1983, Dan had reached and surpassed that goal. He had said in the marriage encounter book that he looked forward to the day when we could finally afford to go out to dinner as a family and when we could go to South Bend for a football game and buy a nice substantial brick house for our family. I gave him more time and I waited, as he asked me to. The sad thing is that by the time he had the money and time for all that, he did it with Linda and not me.

Chapter 16

THE DAYS OF WINE AND ROSES … AND D.U.I.S

Remember the see-saw, the 'it always takes two'? Good, glad you are still with me here.

What I need to reiterate is that all relationships have their ups and downs, that's what commitment is all about: sticking through it even though you feel like you should be 'committed' in the other sense. There are tons of times in a relationship when you want to cry, or leave and divorce, and give up on it all, but then things will get better and you go on. That's what life is about, I think.

Or that's what I thought life was all about. I'm half Italian; the family is all that matters. But now I think that staying too long and trying too hard can end up getting you committed (in a third sense), me being a rather glaring example of this principle.

I wrote in that marriage encounter book that family is all that matters. I believed what I wrote, I meant what I wrote. We had two little girls and then two little boys. We were a real family, although not a perfect family – there is no such thing – but still to this day I believe that family and marriage are sacred institutions. We live our lives, we do our best, we try, fall and get up again, and I think the Japanese were right when they said that, "It's not how many times you fall but

116

how many times you get back up again that matters." In marriage you can work through anything, but only if you both want to. If it's what means the most to both of you. It helps, though, if you can hold hands through it and be best friends to each other.

Dan and I had so much invested in each other. We had been through what seemed like everything together. Four living children, years of college and work and struggles, the death of a child, a house burning down, and three crazy trips across the country so Dan could follow his dreams.

I don't think we were any different than any long-term couple except that maybe we had bigger dreams so we had to work harder and longer than most people do to achieve them. The thing is, all couples, if they stay together long enough, will reach this plateau period in life. During the young years both are struggling to build their futures, often with the wife home with the kids and the husband at work. Both are working hard for the common good, the family. When you hit around forty, you start to wonder where your youth went and what you did with it. You're saddled with the responsibilities of a family and a job. It's an inevitable phase of life, just like the 'terrible twos' are for toddlers. It's like every other phase of your life, it's a time for adjustments.

As for me, Rhett was three and almost in preschool. I didn't want to have another baby and I was ready to move into the next phase of

117

my life, a life beyond pregnancy, babies and diapers. I could have done a lot of things. My first priority was always our family – my husband, our kids, our home – but I felt I could do something while they were at school and work, so I signed up and attended the Accelerated Real Estate School for one weekend.

Dan was totally against it. He refused to babysit while I went to school or when I had to study for the licensing exam. The day of the exam he removed the batteries from my calculator, I guess in the hope I'd fail it. But God Bless all those nuns, because I pencil-whipped that test in record time and passed with no problem.

I was hired by a La Jolla Real Estate firm. Most of the showing of homes I did was on weekends and Dan, as usual, refused to be a babysitter, nor did he want me to hire a babysitter when he was home, so it didn't work out too well. He kept insisting that he wanted me at home where I belonged.

Then I had this great idea for a baby boutique that I was going to call 'Cherubs.' I planned to open it in downtown La Jolla and cater to all the rich grandmas. In addition to having a business of my own, it would give me an excuse to travel to Europe for a buying trip. I was going to carry some French batiste infant clothes at the store. I had a partner lined up, a judge's wife who was into business plans, taxes and bookkeeping. I would play to my strengths – customer service and the front of the store. I really felt that my New York background would be useful here. I had been raised around, and modeled in, some of the most exclusive boutiques and stores in the country. I knew how to do this. We were going to have a signature box and ribbon, much like Bonwit's and Tiffany's did. Those are great because whenever you see one of those boxes you'd know it contained something special and fine. We had the perfect place picked out, too. I was really excited.

And then Dan said, "No." He said, "Even if you make fifty thousand in profit the first year, and you won't, it will all go to taxes and it won't be worth it."

What he really meant was that he didn't want to lose total control over me, but I was fairly anxious by then to have some kind of identity beyond being "his wife and their mom." I wanted to earn my own money again, and with a steady income and the measure of freedom that would come with it, Dan knew, and I knew, that some kind of change had to come. I saw no point in staying home alone all day while the kids were in school and I didn't really enjoy the whole 'ladies who lunch' routine as it seemed somewhat pointless. Once in a while that's great, but I needed a more meaningful existence. I needed to be successful and productive in my own right, and besides, I was concerned about my future and that of the kids following an incident in 1982.

I was home and minding my own business. It was the usual beautiful San Diego weather, and because people don't tend to just drop in in the middle of the day, when the doorbell rang it surprised me. My surprises were only beginning. When I answered the door there was a California Highway Patrolman in full RoboCop regalia, complete with mirrored shades, helmet and high leather boots.

"May I help you?" I asked.

He was all business. "Ma'am do you own a burgundy Jaguar with plates reading DTB III?"

"Yes, we do."

"Where is it?"

I answered that my husband had it.

He said, "Open your garage."

So I did and it wasn't there.

It seems Dan had sideswiped a lady on Freeway 5, by the Sea World exit, earlier that day. After the cop left, I was furious. I had been on Dan for what seemed like forever about his drinking. He drank some alcohol every day and lots of alcohol most days. He always had some after-work function to attend at the Bar Association, or some bar somewhere. Whenever I brought it up, he would tell me that he wasn't an alcoholic because he didn't drink at lunch. Now I had proof that this wasn't true.

I waited and waited for him to come home so I could ask him

about what was so clearly a daytime drinking incident that had led to a hit and run.

Now we have to back up twenty years ... sorry ... to our early days together. Back then, Dan had told me about how his father had been drunk and crashed a plane he was piloting. He also told me about a time when he was a teenager and had been drunk himself and crashed his dad's car. His father had earlier instructed him what to do in the case of just such an occurrence: Leave the scene, go somewhere else, and wait to sober up so they can't get you for driving drunk. Dan told me that he had remembered his father's advice at the time, so he had hidden in the bushes while the cops came to the scene and had walked home afterward. His father had been annoyed about the car but proud of his son for remembering what to do in such a situation.

The San Diego hit and run was not Dan's first adult brush with drunk driving. He was arrested once when the kids were really little. I had to put their sleeping bodies in the car and go and bail him out of jail. A few years after that one I had the adult Fink kids visiting form New York and Dan came home drunk. He proceeded to put on a tuxedo and go out again.

I yelled at him, "If you get arrested tonight, I won't come and get you." Ha, ha, great fun for the whole family. To no one's surprise, but maybe his own, he was duly arrested for drinking and driving.

Fortunately, since the Finks were there, I didn't have to disturb the children. Like a good little wifey, I went and got him off the filthy floor of the drunk tank in downtown San Diego. He had his arm around some guy he was sharing space with and they were chewing gum. Oddly, given all the pathetic events of that evening, I was most struck by him chewing gum. I had never seen Dan chew gum. I remember thinking at the time, 'This isn't how we were raised and I wish I had a camera.'

At other times he'd pass out at parties and I felt like his mother dragging his drunken ass home. I had to stay hyper-sober at parties and evenings out to get him home. I would then lie to the babysitter, drive her home, and get him to bed. This was a fairly regular routine.

Our kids were growing up and beginning to ask questions such as, "What happened to the car? Why is Daddy sick?"

I've always hated lying to anyone – and kids are not stupid – and it seemed to me that they would soon figure out for themselves that Dan had a serious drinking problem.

On the day of the CHP visit, it turned out that Dan had cunningly driven up the hill into Claremont and parked the car behind some cheap motel to hide it, and then checked in until he sobered up and it was safe to come home. That was an important day in our lives because I had finally had enough of his drinking. I thought he was going to kill someone – our kids, himself or an innocent bystander – and for the first time in our marriage I drew a line in the sand.

Dan was horrified and enraged. "How dare you tell me anything!"

New Year's Eve, 1984 – Art Museum Gala. Dan
passed out in the car, leaving Betty there alone
123

He was right, I was breaking our rule, the one he had set down all those years ago on our first date when he had pulled my car over to the side of the road. A lifetime together of him showing me who was boss, and there I was telling him what to do. Nobody told Dan what to do.

That same weekend we were invited to a party at one of the other attorney's houses just down the block in our same neighborhood. I said, "I have an idea. How about we each take responsibility for ourselves. That way I won't feel like your mother and you won't resent me for it. You take your car and I'll take mine." I left first and he never showed up at that party.

The combination of these things opened up the door for Linda, or someone like her, to come in. Dan was scared to death of growing up and turning forty. Peter Pan wanted to stay a young, carefree, party-boy forever, and maybe, too, he was finally cool enough to feel part of a fraternity, like the ones he hadn't been a part of in College. Albeit his fraternity brothers were all middle-aged men with families of their own, but that's just semantics. It's the spirit, or in this case the *spirits*, of the thing that counts.

We had four children and there I was, an ever-present figure expecting him to act his age and show responsibility, and I suppose from his point of view that was grinding. I've always said that Linda just filled the bar stool I didn't want to sit in anymore. We weren't

124

twenty, and as far as I was concerned our days of hanging out at Henny's over Irish coffees, just because, were long gone. I had piano lessons and soccer games and orthodontist appointments, and Linda didn't have any of those. She was available after work to sit beside him in bars and laugh at his jokes and gaze at him like he was a superhero. As for me, I didn't have the time or the inclination anymore to be that girl for him again.

He was my husband and I was his wife, and we had children, and as wonderful as being young and drunk and free with it all before you is, I still thought that being grown up and part of a family with them all around you was even better. Dan obviously felt differently and Linda was right there to remind him that you don't always have to be an adult, you don't always have to do what's right, and sometimes it's okay to just do what you want.

That was her sales pitch and Dan was a very interested buyer.

Chapter 17

EQUITY

We had money by 1982. We could do the things we had wanted to do for a long time. I bought a baby grand piano for Kim and we joined Warner Springs Ranch so the kids could ride on the weekends. We had the money to pay for both but Dan financed them to the hilt anyway.

It's all about equity.

These two items were included in the calculation of the divorce settlement and Dan charged me for their full value, but they weren't paid for.

Over time I've called Dan lots of things, but stupid has never been one of them. Some adjectives that come readily to mind are 'cunning' and 'calculating' and … well, let's leave it here with me simply stating that he was a very smart man.

The first time I heard of Linda was at a birthday party during the '82-'83 holiday season when I overheard Dan say, "Isn't she beautiful?"

That caught my attention because I had never heard Dan say that about anyone.

I asked him later who he was talking about and he said, "This girl who works in the lobby of my building."

In 1983 the money was pretty much rolling in. I could buy clothes and take the kids to lunch and do all kinds of things. Hallelujah!

I had given him more time as he had asked, and as he had said he had delivered the money, and now I knew he could spend what I really wanted from him – more time with us – and we would do things as a family because we had the money finally. So what possible reason could there be for not enjoying each other and the fruits of all those years of labor?

We started by going out for Chinese food as a family, and the kids and I loved it. Dan would meet us there on the way home from work. It seemed like the horrible pressures of the past were gone and that we had finally, finally made it.

I got him a water-ski boat for Father's Day that year so that he could spend more family time with us. Besides downhill skiing, water skiing was the other sport he really enjoyed, and San Diego is a great place to do it.

But we'd no sooner made it to a safer shore, financially speaking, than Dan wanted to move. It was 1983, he had money, and our tract house was no longer suitable to his new image, and so I began the full-time search to find a real custom home in one of the older, more gracious neighborhoods of San Diego.

I searched in La Jolla, Mission Hills and Coronado, and I found several homes that were gorgeous and would have worked.

Dan didn't like any of them.

He also laid down a new edict: no more parties in our present home. He said he was embarrassed to "be living in a tract house."

Betty at the Brodericks' last annual Christmas party, 1982

The children and I were very happy there, but of course we were willing to move to an even nicer home. However, there were big drawbacks to moving, too, because the older houses I was looking at didn't have three-car garages and five large bedrooms with big closets, like our house had, and they didn't have swimming pools, and we had just had one built in the backyard. There were newer quality custom homes with all of these features, but they were very expensive and Dan was very cheap, so it was kind of a problem.

Eventually I found what seemed to be the perfect house for us. It was in Coronado, a very large, seriously regal house. In fact it could be called a mansion. It was right next to the beach and it had amazing potential and lots of property around it. That's not a usual thing in Coronado.

Coronado is safe and clean, and has great schools, and was very close to Dan's downtown office. This time Dan agreed with me. He wrote the check and we were on our way to Coronado.

I was ecstatic and so were the kids. Well, anyone would have been. Coronado is a pretty legendary place and the home of the famous Hotel Del Coronado. In fact I had already started thinking about taking a job there. The Hotel Del was within walking distance and I figured my years at Schafft's in New York were going to come in handy as an event planner there.

I had already worked out the house's decoration and measured for furniture when Dan had an argument with the home's seller. Dan called him an "asshole" and decided to back out of the deal. I tried to change his mind. I told him, "Dan, we won't be living with this man. It's the house. Please, who cares if the owner is an asshole? When it's ours, you'll be the owner."

He wouldn't budge and we didn't buy the house.

Nonetheless, he continued to insist that we could not have people over to our home and he still wanted to move, so I went back onto the house search again. What I didn't understand then, but learned later, is that during all the ultimately vain searching, and even the buying and subsequent backing out of the Coronado house, Dan was already with Linda and he couldn't make up his mind as to whether she should stay or go. I think, in the end, the house search was mostly a smokescreen while he decided what he wanted to do, and if he went he didn't want to leave me and the kids in a place he considered his dream home.

I had already begun to suspect he was having an affair but, of course, he was refusing to admit it.

I wouldn't call it a good time. I had to keep living, though. I had four children to care for and had to try and give them the happiness they deserved. One of the ways I did that was to take the kids camping every summer. We usually went to the Sierras and hiked, and we always enjoyed it. Dan never came because he said he was too busy at work, and besides camping with four kids was not his idea of a good use of his precious leisure time.

In 1983 I decided to take the kids on a 'Grand Tour' of the National Parks of the West. We could afford it, finally, and Rhett was four, so he was old enough to enjoy it, and Kim was thirteen, so better to do it now before the idea of family vacations didn't sound so good to her anymore.

We left on their last day of school and we were scheduled to come back for an important wedding in July. We had the best time. It was a lot of work for me, lifting and loading gear onto the roof and doing all the driving, and though I truly love my kids and their company, I was longing for adult company and conversation too.

Dan flew in twice to meet us, once to Keystone, Colorado, and again to the Flathead Lake Lodge Dude Ranch in Montana. I called home often and got no answer. When Dan flew to Colorado to meet up with us for the weekend, he acted strangely. I figured he was just tired and overworked, as usual, but whatever it was, he wasn't much fun. When he came to Flathead Lake he was so cold and distant that I blew up at him. By then I was really tired of doing everything by myself and I was looking forward to a little help and some companionship. But as soon as he arrived he headed straight to the bar by himself, same-old same-old.

I wanted both of us to be contributing toward this marriage. I couldn't run the big Catholic family of my dreams by myself. I had given him more time, like he had asked for, and since he'd achieved the goals that he had said were holding him back from family intimacy, I expected more from him at last.

Dan apparently saw things rather differently. Yes, he had reached his goals, but from his view from the top, when he looked over our lives, he found that he hated everything about it. All of a sudden he did not like our house – in fact he did not like anything we had built together – and he wanted to throw it away and start over again with a younger new wife, one who hadn't known that earlier man, the poor struggling student, husband and father. With a new woman, the one he already had waiting, their history would begin with the man who mattered to him, handsome, rich and successful, born again you might say, and this time from the top.

Dan, wishing to share his sense of misery and entrapment with me – just in case I was unaware of it and might, even worse, have been somewhat pleased with life – announced to me that, "Seven different women asked me out for my birthday."

I wouldn't bite, so I just answered. "That's nice, Dan."

Annoyed, he expounded on his theme. "You know, women are waiting in line to replace you."

I shook my head and repeated, "That's nice, Dan."

Frustrated by my lack of reaction, he began trying to humiliate me in public by introducing me as "his current wife" at parties. He blamed me for his unhappiness and so, in his mind, everything that followed seemed justified.

Chapter 18

THE DARK YEARS BEGIN

Humpty Dumpty went up a hill; Humpty Dumpty took a great spill. All the king's horses and all the king's men couldn't put poor Humpty Dumpty back together again.

1983 through 1985 were the worst years of my life. They were harder than being dirt poor; they were harder even than being in prison.

Dan attacked and criticized me continually. I suspected something was going on with Linda, so I asked him about it, and he denied it, saying, "No way."

Then he'd follow up the denial by saying I was crazy and imagining things.

At the end of the kids' and my camping trip in the summer of '83, we had car trouble in Las Vegas. I tried to call Dan at home and at work. He wasn't either place day or night. It was very strange. I needed money to get the car repaired, so I kept calling. I think that was my first serious hint that something was up with him.

When we did finally get home, Dan was downright rude to me. On our way to the wedding in the car, he told me how unhappy he was

134

with our lives as they were. He wouldn't admit to an affair and he didn't ask for a divorce, but it was a very bad time. He was horrible to live with.

That September he came home and told me that he had hired someone to help him out at work. I was thrilled. He totally needed help and he was badly overworked, and I thought that must be at the root of his misery – he was just exhausted.

Then he told me that the person he had hired was Linda. I was aghast.

He gave me some song and dance about how she had been fired and was desperate for work, and he felt he had to help her out. He said nobody else would hire her because she had no credentials or skills, being unable even to type. She had been employed as the directory information assistant in the lobby of his building and she had been fired from her challenging position for dating too many of the men who worked there, which had apparently created a lot of gossip and tension.

Linda had arrived in San Diego when she had followed a boyfriend out west from Atlanta. He had dumped her on arrival and she had been couch surfing in Ocean beach, a somewhat run down section of San Diego.

Dan's story was that she had come crying to him when she had gotten fired – a classic damsel in distress and white knight routine. He

saved her. Her hero. What a magical story! I was moved to tears …
well, I was in tears anyway.

I told him that he had thirty days, until October 1st, to get rid of
her or he needed to get out of our house.

He told me again that I was crazy and that I really needed to see
someone, and, oh by the way, "This is *my* house and if you don't like
something, then *you* can get out."

Despite these touching sentiments he still would not admit to the
affair or ask for a divorce. Why I didn't admit it to myself is a
question that I wish I could answer for you, but to date I've never
managed to answer it for myself, so I apologize for any confusion
there.

Dan and I did not live in a vacuum. Many of the couples we
knew were going through the same things at around forty or so. Don,
always a natural leader in trends, had already left his wife and children
by then. He had gotten out of the tracts as well and was living with his
secretary in a new custom home he had built. Couples were splitting
up left and right, and I didn't want a divorce. I couldn't imagine one,
not then. It was too late, or too early, or, well, I guess I just wanted to
stay married to the only man I had ever loved – and still loved – and
save our family.

To this end I read lots of books on the mid-life crisis and found
out that Dan's was a textbook case, and in most of those cases it

passed in time. I suppose that gave me a sense of hope, false hope as it turned out.

As soon as Dan had reached his goals, he had bought himself a red Corvette and a young girlfriend. Just like he had told me "fools do when they come into big money."

Now, bear in mind that California is a community property state. I owned fifty percent of everything we had, just as Dan had owned fifty percent of everything I had when he came into our marriage with nothing. By this time he and I had several cars and boats, and investments as well as cash. If we did get divorced, I thought I would do fine, at least financially-speaking. In some of my darker moments when I contemplated the possibility of divorce, I would try and take stock of things to make myself feel better, or less scared at least. I'd get the house, the kids, and the money to raise them till they were eighteen. I had my real estate license and my teaching credentials, good health, energy, lots of friends and contacts, and some beautiful clothes and nice furniture.

Yes, I would be fine.

I tried to be optimistic in case of either scenario. I used to make a joke about it: "If my husband ever left me, I wouldn't even notice for the first week or two. But if my maid ever left me, I'd be a wreck on the first day." At the time, considering how little Dan was around, it was even sort of true.

137

Whenever Dan and I would argue about his lack of involvement with the kids, he would tell me that as far as they were concerned his job was to, "pay the bills. And I do my job, period, end of discussion."

I'd tell him, "Well, if you really feel that way about it, why don't you leave and just send us the checks?"

These were pointless, sad, mean little arguments that went nowhere, just like the ones we had on our endless searches for a new house. We were spinning in circles and couldn't reach across our individual anger, pain and disappointments to try and find each other. But then, I wasn't something he cared about looking for.

Dan let his new-found wealth go straight to his head and started spending money like water. This was the birth of his so charming alter ego, his self-proclaimed status as royalty, title included. Goodbye Dan Broderick and hello 'Count Du Monay'!

One day the 'Count' drove out to a new development called Fairbanks Ranch and dropped over a million in cash in an afternoon, buying two separate lots. This allowed him to become a charter member the Country Club, which hadn't yet been built. All this was done with nary a whisper of it to me. When I did find out, I said that there was no way that I was moving inland to a place that was going to be a hard hat construction area for the next ten years or so. I already felt like I lived in the car, shuttling the kids back and forth to various school, sports and social activities, as well as dentists etc., and moving out there would have been disastrous. There were no grocery stores, schools, or services of any kind built yet, and the commute back and forth for Dan would have been much longer than the one he already had and already hated, and given him even less time at home. It seemed nuts to me.

Clearly the Count was not thinking straight.

Dan's 40th birthday, November 22nd 1984

All through 1983, 1984 and into 1985, Dan was switching around the finances in preparation for leaving us and I had no clue what he was up to. I still believed – probably because I wanted to believe it so badly – that we would get through this little mid-life crisis and come out on the other side.

It was truly astounding the things he did. The lawyers at Gray, Cary had a booklet they had made up. It was entitled, 'Steps to be taken when preparing to divorce.' I found out about it from Don's ex-wife when they were divorcing, those crafty little devils.

Step #1 was *don't ever let the other party know what you are up to*. Since Dan had exclusive control over our finances, this part was easy for him as I had no way of knowing what he was up to.

I've gone ahead and skipped over some of the juicy stuff that happened in '83 after Dan hired Linda. I've never seen the movies the D.A. made about my life but I've heard she uses one of these incidents in it.

Back at the ranch, October 1st came and went, and Linda was still working for Dan. He would neither get rid of her nor get out. Linda, for her part, was doing fine. She was his first and only full-time employee and had health and dental benefits, unlike poor Sharon who had worked faithfully for Dan for years as a private contractor.

To reward Linda for her special skill set, Dan had put her in the very expensive new office next to his, instead of making her hide her light under a bushel in a windowless cubicle, like the one Sharon had.

Clearly Sharon was just not the performer Linda was. Clearly neither was I.

November 7th, 1983, was my thirty-sixth birthday. I bought a Baskin Robbins ice cream cake because they were my kids' favorites and we waited for Dan to come home for dinner. Six, seven, eight and nine pm came but Dan didn't.

The kids had some cake and I put them to bed. We left the candles on the cake and took pictures, which is the best part of a birthday anyway.

Ten o'clock came and still no Dan, not even a phone call. I have to say that Dan was never overtly romantic or affectionate, but he was never as cold as this. He was still telling me that I was crazy. Well, in part he was right; he was making me crazy with all his lies.

I hate it when people lie to your face, because that means they have so much contempt for you. They think you are so stupid and pathetic that you will believe anything. I'm not stupid. I knew about Linda from Day 1. I knew they were lovers before he hired her. People had seen them out together and told me about it every time.

That night, my birthday, was the second time I attempted suicide. This time I not only took all the pills I could find but I slit my wrists with a razor blade. Whatever the D.A. said about this being a halfhearted attempt, let me assure you I meant it. My heart was broken and I did not want to live anymore.

It didn't work. Nothing I did worked in those days. I woke up again in plenty of time to make the sailing trip our neighbors had planned for my birthday. I looked horrible in the pictures and probably worse in person, and I had these humiliating bandages on my wrist that I kept trying to cover up, but fortunately Dan was in fine form and I don't think anyone noticed a thing out of place.

November 22nd was Dan's birthday. My friends Vicki and Wilma knew how concerned I was about Linda, and they told me to get dressed up and go down to his office and surprise him. I was never encouraged to go to Dan's office – in fact quite the opposite – but I did it.

I had brought him a brass telescope on an oak tripod so he could watch the aircraft carriers come and go out of San Diego Bay. I thought he'd like that. I also got him, as a semi-joke, a pretentious second gift: a twenty-four carat gold tire pressure gauge for his new midlife crisis Corvette.

When I arrived at his office, Dan wasn't there.

What were there were remnants of cake and balloons. I noticed that he had taken several of our wedding crystal glasses to the office and there was an empty champagne bottle on his desk. Remember how Dan was about not having had a party for his first office? Well, evidently things had changed.

Dan had a stunning one hundred-and-eighty degree ocean view

143

from his office and I sat down in his burgundy leather nail head office chair, the one I had custom-ordered for him, and stared out at that view while not really seeing it.

I called Vickie and told her what I had found and how the lobby receptionist had told me, "They went out to lunch and never returned."

Vickie asked me, "What are you going to do?"

I told her I didn't know and hung up the phone.

Then I formulated a plan. If he wouldn't get rid of Linda or move out, I'd just move him out myself!

Dan had said to me once that there was nothing that he needed or cared about if he ever left beyond his checkbook and his car. Well, he had those with him.

I went home and walked directly into our bedroom. Once there I took armfuls of his precious dandy clothes and threw them over the balcony off our room into the backyard. It still kind of burns me – pardon the pun – that despite being more upset than I can describe, and as angry as I've ever been in my life, I still couldn't bring myself to burn his very favorite things, like his damned cape and top hat, or the straw boater hat he loved.

When I had finished throwing all his clothes into the back yard, I got gasoline from the garage and set them on fire. My friends Vicki and Wilma were there, and to my eternal regret, all of my children. I can't excuse doing it in front of them. There is no excuse. All I can say is that I was literally beside myself that night. By that I mean I felt as though I were standing apart from the sobbing woman and watching it through a viewfinder: her burning her husband's clothes, her burning life.

Dan didn't come home until much later. He didn't call either, which is probably best in hindsight as I have no idea what I would have said to him.

Like the endlessly hopeful pleaser that I am, and despite the ugliness of my own birthday a few weeks before, I had still made a special birthday dinner for him, in fact the one he had specifically requested: roast beef and a German chocolate cake for dessert.

When Dan finally showed up, he found the front door locked so he went around to the back. He had no idea that I had been to his office earlier and so he was puzzled, or acted that way, and of course he was drunk, which might have dulled his senses a bit more as he tried to pretend that nothing was wrong.

I told him, "You won't move out, so I moved you out myself."

Wilma and Vickie were still there, and all the kids were awake, but he just walked inside the house and went upstairs to bed, without saying one word to any of us. Years later I would ask people, 'Imagine if you really were innocent and you came home to a crazy wife who did that, how would you act?'

145

Betty with close friends Anne Dick, Vickie Currie and Pam Boynton

The next day Dan told me in an annoyed way that he and Linda had simply gone to lunch and then he had left to do depositions and had no idea where she went after that. Poor Dan, poor, poor innocent Dan, the 'martyred lawyer man.' With the crazed wife.

146

Naturally he was still refusing to admit the affair, and despite my insane ways, he remained with me, even repeating his supportive suggestions about my seeking mental health care. The man was a saint, I tell you.

Bear in mind that this was 1983 and we were still living at Coral Reef, and the kids didn't understand what was going on. All they saw was Mommy crying a lot and being tense and short with them – not my usual demeanor and not fair to them. At that point I still didn't believe in telling them. In fact, except with a few close friends, I wasn't talking about it all. I don't know if that made things worse or not for me. There's no handbook out for how to handle this, or there wasn't t that time. Maybe this book can serve as a guide as to what you shouldn't do.

Chapter 19

KEEPING UP APPEARANCES

We canceled our annual family Christmas party in 1983, at Dan's request, to the disappointment of so many people, because coming to our Christmas party had become their own family tradition.

Decorations for the last annual Christmas party, 1982

Since I couldn't tell the real reason why we weren't having it, I gave no explanation. Dan knew I loved having these parties, so maybe that was why he insisted they stop. He didn't say one way or the other.

Meantime, Linda stayed on and Dan kept coming home, albeit late, but he came home. He was busy at work, like always, and busy too with a bunch of financial machinations behind my back. I wanted him to leave or stay, and if he stayed, to really stay, and that meant no more Linda. In the words of the late Princess Diana, "There were three of us in that marriage and it was a bit crowded."

I understood later that Dan was trying to get me to file for divorce in order to appear to be the innocent party. Image and public perception were everything to him. He didn't want people to think he would just up and leave his nice wife and four children for a secretary who couldn't even type. That would make him look like a bad guy, maybe even foolish, and the latter was utterly unacceptable to Dan's world view or the way he needed people to view him, so he had to turn everything around on me and make it become somehow my fault, just as he had done back in 1969 when he had jumped on me for no reason and ended up with a black eye and everybody's sympathy.

I knew what he was doing and I wouldn't help him.

Even when he finally walked out of the rental house two years later, he turned around and said, "Do you want me to leave now or in the morning?" At least by then I'd been married to a lawyer long enough not to fall for his 'heads up I win, tails you lose' lawyer chat routine. He had already announced he was leaving and so either answer I could have given would have made it look like I wanted him to leave. What I did tell him was that he could leave whenever he wanted.

The thing is, Dan always twisted and turned every argument or situation to his advantage. It made him brilliant and lethal in the courtroom and it made me the world's biggest loser in our house, but privately in his heart and head I believe he knew it was wrong, knew that I saw through his every game because I knew him so well and once upon a time we'd been good friends.

In 1983 and 1984 I was dealing with my husband having an affair – or I thought he was but he said he wasn't, and I knew he was but I wanted to believe him – and I see now that a lot of my craziness started then. I didn't know what to do, but at that time I did know I didn't want him to go. Still, I was really mad at him a lot of the time, so some of the things I did were to try and keep him, but other times I just wanted to punish him, and either way it usually blew up in my face.

As you can guess from me burning Dan's clothes and all my mentions of how he dressed, clothes were a big thing with him. They never had been with me. I had always liked beautiful clothes and, being tall, could wear them. I'd had them before we had gotten married, but during our protracted starving student days I'd learned to live without them. If I thought about clothes at all back then, it was to either admire or be furious with Dan at how much he spent on his own clothes and how cheap he was about my kids needing anything new.

So when we first started making money, I began to think about pretty clothes for myself for the first time in years and to buy them too. But it wasn't until New York in the fall of 1983 that I managed to shock even Dan with my clothing choices.

That was no easy thing to do. Remember, this guy had been buying at Barneys back when we couldn't pay our car insurance and this was after Dan had hired Linda and after he had ignored my "Get rid of her by October first or else" ultimatum. He hadn't fired her and I hadn't done anything, and they were going on with their affair downtown and my friends were 'helpfully' calling me up and telling me about seeing them so that, "you won't be embarrassed hearing it from someone else."

I was already flailing by then. That fall – and I can't recall if it was October or early November, I just know it was before that year's Blackstone Ball which is held on November 16th – anyway, we had flown to New York for a couple days.

Dan was so cold to me and it seemed like everything I did made him angry. He didn't want to go anywhere with me, not even to re-

151

visit any of our special old spots or to do anything except sit in the bar and drink. So I had gone off for a walk, and when I came back I found him downstairs in the lobby on the phone. He was talking to Linda.

Betty spent the whole trip in tears, provoked by Dan's cruelty to her

I wanted to pull him off the phone or smash it, or something, but that kind of stuff came later, so I just stood there and looked at him, crying, and he saw me, but he didn't hang up, he just turned his shoulder and kept talking to her in this tone of voice I hadn't heard him use for me in so long.

152

I didn't know what to do, so I turned around and gave him his privacy so that he could talk to his whore. I didn't want to go up to our room, and besides I didn't think he'd follow me up there if I had, and all he'd do was lie and deny everything, so I went outside and up the block to Elizabeth Arden and grabbed this gorgeous lavender and pink kind of mermaid dress off the rack. It was a size 8, so I knew it would fit, and it was on sale for $8,000. I pulled out my credit card and bought it. I'd never done anything like that before.

When I got back to the hotel, Dan had finished his little business call and was in the room. I showed him my new dress with the price tag still on it and he nearly died, which made me feel a little bit better.

That year I had been on the committee for the Blackstone Ball and I had my beautiful new dress and I was pretty excited. Yes, Dan was still with Linda and still lying to me, but I thought maybe if he saw me all dressed up and looking beautiful, he would, I don't know, love me again, like me again, maybe at least tell me that I looked pretty. It's stupid, I know, and it didn't happen.

What did happen was that I spent most of the day primping – hair, nails, makeup, the whole thing – and then I put on my dress and went downstairs to show the kids. They were great about it. "Mommy, you look like a princess."

When Dan came home, he just brushed past me, saying he had to get ready and change.

I asked him if he liked my dress and he just looked at me. "I don't know, Betts. I haven't got time for this. Actually, I don't even want to go, but I have to. You don't, so it seems like a lot of money for nothing."

I started shaking and crying, and ran back up to our bedroom and locked the door.

Dan yelled through it that it was fine with him; he'd just go as he was.

Kim came up and I let her in. She helped me put my makeup back on and I ended up going. Dan never really looked at me all night but one of the guys from the firm said, "Betty, I knew you'd have the best dress at this party. I was just telling my wife that and here you are."

This pink and lavender dress was my first Bob Mackie evening gown. I bought another one for the Blackstone in 1984. 1984 had been a horrible year and why I thought that another expensive dress would make Dan want me I have no clue about. All I can say is I still wanted him then and I wanted him to want me, and maybe I thought there was some magic ingredient in clothes that could do that, who knows?

Anyway, I knew Dan loved his stupid cape, the one I hadn't been able to burn the year before, and his cape was red and black, so I spent weeks looking for the most beautiful dress I could find that would match his cape.

The one I got was a gorgeous, strapless red and black Bob Mackie, and once again I spent the day primping, and this time I didn't just work on me. I got the house ready for a photographer I'd hired to capture Dan and I in what I was sure would be this romantic couple scene picture that I could treasure forever. Well, I still have the picture.

Dan came home rushed and late again, and he didn't say one word about my dress, he just went upstairs and primped, but at least when he came down he was wearing the cape. I asked him to come into the living room and stand by me for a picture in front of the vase of red roses I had put there.

The photographer seemed scared of Dan too, since he was glaring at him and hadn't said a single word. I leaned forward and flipped Dan's cape back to show the red lining, and tried to kiss him, but he flinched back and I stepped back and stared straight ahead. There we were in all our glory, the unhappiest couple in the world, and we had made it, we had everything and we had nothing, but at least we were well dressed for it, like at a funeral.

Chapter 20

2014

If the letters I get are any indication, people have wanted to hear this story from me for a long, long time, but there are many reasons why I chose not to tell it earlier.

Number one was that, despite what has happened, I am not a public person. The D.A. tried to turn me into one, and I suppose in terms of name recognition she succeeded, but that was her choice, and the media's choice, not mine. I was a housewife and Dan was a lawyer, and this was simply a domestic abuse case like thousands of others that you never hear about. I didn't understand then why that would be of much interest. I do now; at least I think I do.

Dan and my story played into a lot of people's deepest fears which resulted in their projecting themselves into our lives. It was our very ordinariness that made us extraordinary, or rather made us extraordinarily topical. If it could happen to us, who had all the same hopes, successes, failures and problems that they did, and it went this wrong, then could it happen to them? Well, sure it could, but if you're sitting at home reading this, it probably didn't and that makes it even better, because it's interesting from a distance. Up close it's like being in Hell.

The second reason I haven't done this earlier is my kids. They don't need any more attention from this case. It was all such a long time ago and we have all tried very hard to move beyond it.

The third reason was that I can't tell this story without naming names of who did what, and most of the people we knew were lawyers. If you even mention a lawyer's name, they want to sue you, even if what you say is the irrefutable truth. I don't want to deal with lawyers ever again.

These are my words, my recollections, my memories and my story. There is still freedom of speech in this country and I want to tell my story now. I'm sixty-seven years old and I want my kids to know what really happened. I would never sell my story, not to anyone, and every penny I make on this book will be split evenly among the real victims of the case, our four children. And, before I move on, or better to say move backwards, I want to address the inevitable question that my last sentence will bring up: "Don't you want to give reparation to *all* the victims of this story?"

I'm sorry to answer with a question, but I have to ask, "Who else?"

If by 'victims' you mean Dan's family, well then I can only think you mean Larry Broderick, who has benefited financially both before and after Dan's death, and I do not see him in the same classification as my children. If you mean Dan's parents, they are gone now and beyond my apologies for their loss, as I am beyond their forgiveness.

If you mean Linda's family, contrary to what anyone might think, I have great remorse and guilt. I didn't like her in life and to say otherwise would be to lie, but I should not have taken her life. That was a horrible and demented, sickening and wrong thing to do, and I do understand, in as much as one can understand another's grief, the agony I have caused her family. If I could change what happened, I would. Obviously I can't. And if money mattered to her family, they have certainly never given any sign of it. When Larry cut Linda's family from Dan's will and life insurance, on the premise that since Dan died last they were entitled to nothing, that was him not me. Their graceful decision to accept that makes them better than I would have been in their position. That Larry billed them for Linda's casket was again not me. Yet it was me who caused them to be in their situation. I know that Larry did not kill that young woman. What I'm trying to say, and probably saying badly, is that if I thought money would help their grief I would split it five ways, but it seems as though they are above, or maybe beyond, that and always have been. What they wanted, and I'm sure still do want, is Linda back. What they want is for Linda to have returned to her the life I took.

In ending her life, I destroyed my own as well, though at the time I thought she and Dan had already ended mine. I know now that is not true. I get to see my children still and hear their voices and see the sky, and those are not small things. Nothing in this life is a small thing.

At the time I could not see that; I could only see that the family and the life I loved were gone. It felt to all intents and purposes that I was already dead, and in that terrible second, not valuing any kind of life, I took both of theirs. I am sorry, and I have remained and will remain sorry all the days of my life, but despite my grief and guilt I am still here, and being here I want to tell my story.

Chapter 21

DANCING FROM STRINGS

Now back to the story, and to my mind the juicy part. Without this, the rest of it is only the tale of a messy mid-life, ho-hum, boring divorce saga. What sets our little tragic tale apart, I believe, is the massive legal crap storm that went on after Dan left in 1985.

By then, whether you doubt it or not, I had real moments where I was happy to be rid of him. The previous two-plus years had been misery for us and our innocent children because of the never-ending lies and the fights caused over Linda. Of course I was sad that my dream of a happy family life was over, but I am a survivor and I thought the kids and I would be fine in time. At the beginning I fully expected a quick, quiet divorce settlement.

I was aware that Dan was in a position to cheat me big-time, since I didn't have a clue how much money we had or where it was, and I didn't much care at that point. I just wanted enough money to continue to live the life we had and raise the children with the life they were used to, until they went to college. All my kids were always good students and I fully expected that they would end up at top-flight universities. I did not want to fight with Dan or argue over anything – this was his affair and his divorce – and it seemed logical to me that

162

he would want it over as quickly as possible too.

Part of his 'preparations for divorce' was to get rid of anything I had equity in. By the time Dan walked out the door, he had managed me into a temporary rental home, because the Coral Reef house had a crack in the foundation, and into a leased car, leaving me zero equity in either a home or a car. When he first left, I had no idea where he had gone, but it turned out that he had returned to take possession of our Coral Reef house, even though it was in an unlivable condition. As he had told me back in the long-ago Harvard Law days, "possession is nine tenths of the law."

The lease on the rental house we were using while the Coral Reef house was repaired was for the school year of September 1984 through June 1st of 1985. The kids and I were fine there. I wrote to the owners to ask if we could stay on beyond June 1st and they said they were happy with that. However, there was a problem. Home owners insurance, and not Dan, had been paying for the lease of the rental house for that first year while the Coral Reef house was being repaired. When the insurance was up after the Coral Reef house became livable again, the payments needed to come from Dan, but Dan wasn't having it. No way was he going to pay to have us stay on there, nor did he have any intention of letting me back into the Coral Reef house either.

It took Dan from 1983 to 1985 to finagle possession of the

163

jointly-owned Coral Reef family home from me, and he was a tricky, deceitful little weasel in his handling of this. Meantime he was maintaining his public façade and no one had any idea what was going on with us.

Christmas at the rental house, 1984

Dan was always calm and cool and collected. He had no problems. All the problems now belonged to me one hundred percent as I tried to build a life beyond my marriage to him.

May 1985 was my Dad's seventieth birthday and there was a big shindig that they had planned back in New York. My entire extended family would be there and I felt I had to go. Even more, I wanted to go – I badly needed to be around my family at that time – but no children were invited to that party. It was a strictly adults-only affair. I could have left the children at home under the supervision of a sitter, but there was another problem: our rental house had just become infested with a plague of rats, and which sitter would have put up with rats skittering all around them continuously? I shouldn't have put up with it myself. The kids and I were terrified of being there. We could hear those rats running around squeaking all night long. It was horrible.

The upstairs bedrooms of the Coral Reef house had never needed any work doing to them, so I wanted to propose putting the kids back with Dan for a week while I went to New York. When Dan had left there had been no agreement about how much money he would give me or when he would see the kids, and during all of February, March and April he had given me no money whatsoever, nor would he take any of my calls at his office.

He had come over once, on St Patrick's Day, and I let him spend the night. I thought maybe we could talk in the morning, when he was sober, about our separation and getting back together, and the kids and money, but he left before I woke up. There would have been no point in trying to discuss any of this when he showed up, because he was drunk. Worse, I didn't even try, because I was glad to see him. I thought it meant he missed me, like I missed him, and I went to bed with him because it felt like maybe he loved me again. But he didn't and it was a mistake, a mistake I think a lot of women in my position make.

He didn't take my calls all the following week either.

There's a book out called 'Crazy Time' about divorce, and, speaking for myself, this really was crazy-making because Dan was still lying about his relationship with Linda, claiming he wanted to sell the Coral Reef house and get somewhere else nice together with me and the kids.

In the meantime he found a two-story replica of his father's house near Balboa Park and he wanted us to move there. Back then it was a bad part of town. We called it the 'Gay Ghetto' because there were gay bars and bath houses with peep shows. I hear it's much nicer now but in those days it was no place to move young children to. It didn't make any sense to me. Why would we leave La Jolla? It had the beach, the kid's school and their friends, so why would we want to move away from all of that? I refused to even go see the house because I didn't care what it looked like inside; I didn't want my children there. Location is everything.

Photo of Dan's new house, taken from Betty's car

Dan bought the house anyway. He got a "great deal" because no one else wanted a mansion in the slums. Of course I didn't even know he had bought it; he didn't tell me, just like he didn't tell me what he was doing with 'our' money, which he considered 'his' money alone.

It wasn't until I returned from New York in mid-May of 1985 that I found out Dan had written one of his intimidating legal missives to the owners of the rental house, telling them that we would "be adhering to the original terms of the lease."

What that meant to me in practical terms was that I had to get out of the rental house and that I had nowhere to go because Dan didn't

167

want me to come and live in the Coral Reef house, even though it was as much my house as his. In fact he had gotten a restraining order to keep me away from my house and my four children on the basis that I had come by one afternoon in May to see the kids, and had misbehaved.

There was a Boston Crème Pie on the kitchen counter. I asked the sitter who had made it, because it looked like something one of the kids would have made.

She answered, "Linda."

I said, "Linda who?"

"You know, Dan's girlfriend Linda."

She was in my house with my kids, and Dan was still trying to pretend there was nothing between them? What a jerk! I lost it and smeared the cake on the bedspread in our bedroom, my bedroom.

Of course Dan, being an attorney, blew the damages from my cake escapade through the roof and wanted to charge me four hundred dollars. That seemed a little over the top. I mean, exactly how much damage can you do with one crappy little cake, even if you are really, really angry, and I was?

So that's what he used to get the restraining order, barring me from coming into my own house, but I know I reacted poorly to seeing that cake. I should have risen above it, but I couldn't, or I didn't, or maybe during that period nothing else seemed possible to me but letting myself lose control. I know Dan hated me for it. I hated myself for it. I hated him too. Most of all I hated what I had become, what had become of us.

Dan had a lot of catchy phrases he used to use when telling me about all the dirty tricks he used in his cases. One of them was "Get 'em by the short hairs and twist." Another one was, "Don't start negotiating until you're sitting on their face." His mantra was to surprise the other side and to hardball, and in the world of litigation scorched earth is not considered a negative thing.

Now I was watching him do all those same things to me. *Why?*

I asked myself that for years, then I read 'The Kite Runner,' and I understood 'defeated guilt' for the first time.

One time Dan told me about a particularly ugly thing he did to humiliate, harass and threaten some poor doctor, smiling gleefully as he recounted the details. It seems the guy was a leading member at his church, so Dan had sent the process servers to slap him with his lawsuit while he was seated in the front row of the church with his wife and children. Dan considered this to be one of his finer moments.

Years later, when Dan decided to serve me with divorce papers, he wanted to do it in a similar way. Lee attended the Bishops School in La Jolla and I was very active in the parents club there. We had one big auction fashion show each year and I was on the committee that did the luncheon. So Dan gave the process server a photo of me and

169

sent him to the event to subject me to the maximum of humiliation and public upset. It didn't work out, though. Every woman in La Jolla, it seems, is blond, and most of them were there that day, so the guy couldn't identify me. I only found out about this because Dan was keeping a dated diary about what I did and I saw the notation 'attempted service at the Bishops Luncheon.' Since I was home 99% of the time, Dan had to wait and go to a lot of trouble and extra expense to plan his surprise hardball attack on me. Maybe he felt badly that it didn't work out, but what would it have mattered in the end? You can only bruise someone in so many places, after all.

It was around that time that I started calling him an 'asshole' to his face. Me doing that drove him crazy. Dan was a serious control freak and he had lost all control of me. Of course, the downside was that I had also lost all control of me too. I was so angry at him for all his lies, I had started to refuse to do anything he wanted me to do. He was out of my life and I had a right to do my own thing, away from his obsessive-compulsive need to control me. This particular struggle went on for years beyond our split in 1985.

I had stopped going to Al-Anon meetings after Dan left me – I was no longer living with an alcoholic – and I started going to 'A Course in Miracles' meetings instead. Al-Anon's message was "detach, detach, detach," whereas the 'Course in Miracles' said to never defend yourself against an attack. I did not want to fight, argue, or go to court with Dan Broderick. I wanted us to sit down like two at least semi-rational adults and deal out our cards. It really didn't matter to me if I got half of our assets, not that I would have had a clue what my 'half' comprised anyway. I just wanted what I needed to raise the kids.

Betty in 1985, after Dan left her

My offer to him was that I would accept one million dollars cash in the bank and twenty-five thousand dollars a month in taxable family support for me and the four kids. Considering how much money was pouring in by then, that was both conservative and fair.

He refused to accept this offer, nor would he counter it with one of his own. As far as he was concerned, he had no reason to ever settle with me. My life was entirely on hold pending a settlement, while his life never skipped a beat. He had possession of all our assets, and of our children, and of our house and the furniture inside of it. My life was in a shambles and his was going along according to plan, *sans* me.

Dan, and later the D.A., tried to paint me as a crazy woman who wanted him back. That was the last thing I would have ever wanted! Onlookers had no idea what was really going on in the sealed, secret, crooked court rooms of San Diego.

Linda sent me a photo of him and her together before he even filed for divorce. The typed Post-it attached to the photo said, "IT MUST KILL YOU TO SEE THESE TWO HAPPY TOGETHER. EAT YOUR HEART OUT BITCH!!"

Linda wasn't much easier on me than Dan was.

I didn't understand it then, and in some ways I still struggle with it today. I had never done anything to her. She didn't know me. I was going down for the count a little more each day and she was throwing ever more stones at me. It has always been hard for me to fathom what motivated her to be so gratuitously cruel.

There were a load of gold diggers like her operating in downtown San Diego in those days and for all I know the next generation is still there today. They hung out at the offices and the bars, and sniffed around the lawyers day and night, flirting and promising and stroking their immense egos. I was shocked that Dan fell for her act but I guess forty-year-old men are vulnerable to young pretty girls on the make who will say and do anything they think the older – and always richer – man wants from them. What's not to love about a set-up like that? Except in how it affects the older man's wife and kids, I mean.

Meantime, I wasn't at the bars being sucked up to by good looking young gigolos. I was busy trying to find a lawyer to represent me against Daniel T. Broderick III in a very tight-knit legal community, and I wasn't succeeding.

As part of his 'Steps to be taken when preparing for a divorce,' he had gone out of his way to befriend the few top-notch divorce lawyers that there were in town. Dan was playing chess and he had all his pieces in a row to checkmate me at every turn. Our divorce was the most important case of his life and he knew he had to ensure that he won it. It was time to call in every favor that any judge had ever owed him, and he did.

While we were still together and still living at the Coral Reef house back in 1983, Dan had come home in an unusually good mood one evening. I asked him why he was so happy and he said it was because he just got assigned the judge he had asked for in a big case.

When I looked confused, he said, "I know now I've got it won."

I said, "I thought the jury decided on a case."

He answered, "Nope, the whole outcome of a case depends on what evidence a judge will or will not let in."

Ironically, one of the reasons that I'm sitting in prison twenty-five years after the killings is for just that reason. In my criminal proceedings the judge would not allow the battered women expert who had testified in my first trial to repeat his testimony in the second. I think, without hearing expert testimony, that it was very hard for the jury to understand my state of mind and how I thought at that time, and how those thoughts led to the killings. For some reason, my defense lawyer, Jack Earley, did not apply to stop my second trial but instead proposed summoning a different expert when the one he had previously used quit in total disgust and frustration. So it turns out Dan was right.

The other thing that can really cost you in a trial is judges' discretion. To give an example of how that little sleight of hand goes, let me address Epstein Credits. Dan charged me a million dollars' worth of them in our divorce trial. The law specifically states that

Epstein Credits are not to be used to dilute community property, the community of the marriage. But ultimately that call rests with the judges' discretion. Judge Howatt allowed Dan to illegally claim Epstein Credits to wipe out my entire half of our community property. Judges' discretion, indeed.

It went the same way with custody of the children. I did not want to wage a custody battle and get in the mud with Dan. Custody battles are disgusting and tear everyone to pieces, and we were doing that so well already without needing to bring in outside help. It was obvious who the 'primary parent' was. The boys repeatedly told judge after judge that they wanted to live with me. There was nothing Dan could use against me, either personally or as a parent, but he got sole custody, with no visitation allowed for me, and he got it from a judge without there even being a hearing. To me that was the same as if he had kidnapped them at gunpoint. There was no legal justification or basis for that order, just like there was no legal justification for Dan to have the court appoint an 'elisor' to forcefully sell the Coral Reef house without my knowledge or consent, but it happened anyway.

God help me, all I could think, and that's when I could think, was *What is going on here?* I was through the looking glass and day-by-day becoming as mad as the hatter at the tea party. I was forced into sealed, secret, private courtrooms time after time, and always against my wishes, while my protests were ignored. After all, Dan had to make sure that nobody knew what he was doing. Every time I tried to get help from anyone, he would tell them, "Don't listen to her, she's crazy."

Meantime, the months and the years were going by, and during that time I hired several lawyers who took my money while Dan made fools out of them in the courtrooms.

We lost every time.

I was fine in 1985 when he left. I was still fine in 1986. I understood that these things took time. But by 1987 I had fallen into a serious depression.

Dan had me jailed for "stepping a foot onto his property," which violated his restraining orders, and for calling him names, and during it all what pounded the hardest in my head was what I was missing with my children. Years of their lives, every event large and small, was denied me. Dan had even told their schools not to allow me on the grounds, not this dangerous, crazy woman.

The headmaster, who had known me for years, was sympathetic but afraid that Dan would sue the school if he violated his orders. Everyone was always so afraid of Dan Broderick. They weren't scared that he would punch or slap them like some street thug – he was much more terrifying than that. His weapon was the court system and that is a weapon that can destroy an entire life in a bad hour. I know there are other weapons. I'm here because of that, and what I did is inexcusable, but I didn't start that war, and by the time I finished it, I truly believed I was a casualty. I fired that gun from the bottom of a trench. I'm not saying this to excuse myself – I killed two people, I understand that – but then, oh then, I was fighting for my life, and in my head, where all the terror and rage had coalesced and wiped out everything else, all that was left was the kind of sick desperation that drives suicide bombers.

Brad Wright

Long before I snapped, back when I was just running in place trying to find help, I didn't think I was paranoid or crazy for being afraid of Dan, because everyone else was too: Brad, my boyfriend after Dan and I divorced, was scared of Dan; my dad was scared of Dan; apparently every doctor and lawyer in Southern California was scared of Dan as well; but only I was considered insane for saying it out loud.

It still puzzles me that when this case happened and I said, "I lived in terror and fear of his next attack on me," everyone shook their heads and thought, 'Poor crazy Betty.'

Crazy or not, it was the truth.

Dan said in a newspaper interview, "This won't be over until one of us is gone." I knew he meant it, and it scared me. I could never be free of him, I *would* never be free of him, or that is how I felt, and when you are in terror, perception is your only reality.

Dan used his legal weapons to pound me into the ground over and over from 1985 until the day that I killed him on November 5th 1989, and again that was a heinous crime that I committed, but, until he died, Dan was relentless in his destruction of me and I felt he would never stop. He had said he would never stop.

Linda was no innocent bystander in that mess either. She was a very active in her partnership with Dan. Linda is the one who put the house's answering machine on the children's phone to keep me from being able to talk to them in 1985, after she and Dan and the kids moved into the house in Balboa Park. There was never an order that I couldn't speak with my children. My children loved me and they relied on me for everything, even though they weren't living with me. They were as afraid of setting off Dan's temper as I had always been, and so, if they had a problem or needed something, they called me. I was still their primary parent.

To me it seemed that Linda wanted to be me and that was impossible to do unless she first erased me, then she wouldn't be a sequel, she'd be the only one – Dan's only love and wife, his children's mother. But to make that real, or at least real to her, I couldn't exist anymore. To make it *really* real, not only did I have to go but so did my memory. And it's weird, but if I can take myself out of this (like she and Dan wanted), I can almost get why they felt that way.

For Dan I think I was just this living reminder that he hadn't started out as this very handsome, seriously successful 'master of the universe,' to borrow from Tom Wolfe. The Dan of the days of Linda was fairly untouchable in terms of looks, money, power, and the respect and control that I think he had thought was his due from birth. Yet I was around to remind him of the broke, skinny, nerdy, insecure young guy he had been, and I was a dark mirror he wanted gone.

For Linda it was even worse than that. He was her knight in

179

shining armor, and that armor was pretty shiny when she met him. She was young and in love, and he was like this living embodiment of what any girl would dream of, up to and including the existence of his four beautiful, intelligent kids. But there I was to say he hadn't always been this way and that those beautiful children weren't just his, and so now hers, all alone. I was this very loud reminder that there had been someone before her and that maybe being with Dan wasn't going to be quite the dream that she wanted it to be.

I mean, what the Hell? How could her Prince Charming have ever been married to this old, loud, wrinkled, ever-fatter wreck, 'this woman in ruins,' as Bella Stumbo was later to call me with some accuracy. I must have been as horrible a premonition of her future as she was a painful reminder of what I had lost to become the woman she now so wanted to be. This was especially awkward in the case of the four kids, and so that was where she sought to hit me hardest.

In those days, whatever her motivations, all I could see was that she seemed to be copying me. She started wearing the same clothes I did, or had before I got too fat for them, but with shorter skirts because I had gotten too old for them. She ordered the same personalized stationary I had had, with the same name I used to have before I'd gotten too divorced for it. She wanted the same car I drove and the same life I'd had with Dan ... well, after he'd started making money. I don't think she would have liked the basement apartments much, but never mind.

What's funny now to me is this: Dan had dumped me, and he claimed that he not only despised me then but had always hated me, so I don't know, I'm no psychologist, but maybe she should have avoided copying the thing he hated most, and I wish I'd been less crazy then so I could have said that to her.

There are all these graves in Ireland, and their headstones sort of sum up me and Linda:

Stop traveler and cast an eye
As you are now so once was I.
Prepare in time, make no delay.
For youth and time will pass away.

Or I like this one too:

Once I stood where you do now.
And viewed the dead as you do me.
Before long you'll lie as low as I
And others will come and look on thee.

Sorry I'm getting morbid in my old age, but really you do learn the older you get to take a little more care of not just yourself but of other people, if for no better reason than that we all end up in the same place.

It's hard, though, when you're young, I know that. I didn't look very hard at Dan either, and so I'm sorry I judged Linda so harshly for her own blind faith in his every word, including those he said about me. I wasn't where I am now in terms of all the vast hindsight of wisdom that twenty-five years in prison have given me. I was right in the middle of the classic cat fight, and I could scratch back too.

Before they moved in together, he had bought her a condo in Mira Mesa. I told everyone that Mira Mesa was a dump, adding that, "If you're gonna keep a ho, at least keep her somewhere classier."

But the truth is twofold: One, he had bought her that 'dump' with our money and I resented that pretty badly; and, two, dump or not, it was an awful lot nicer than anyplace he had kept me and my kids in for the first decade or so of our lives together.

When she wanted a Jaguar like mine, Dan didn't buy her that but he did get her a new Toyota. I made fun of it too, calling it a cheap knockoff car, but again the real truth was that he'd used our money and I was remembering my long-ago-stolen little MG and all those years on buses.

Next she wanted a fur coat and I laughed because he picked her up a "cheap tacky fox jacket" from May Co. How pathetic, right? Or maybe not so much, since yet more of our community property money was used and it had taken fifteen years of marriage before I ever got a fur, and then I'd had to buy it myself. In retrospect both Linda and I look pathetic here. Furs in San Diego ... kind of desperate, wasn't it?

Then he got her teeth fixed with, you guessed it, our money. I found that one out because he used our family orthodontist.

Even before the condo, car, fur and teeth, he had, it turns out, gotten her a credit card, right back at the beginning, in 1983. She was allowed to use it anywhere she wanted, though Dan told me it was for business only. Even I'm not that stupid, nor am I forgetful. I remembered the scenes about buying a ten dollar dress I wanted, or new shoes for our kids, or that damn bathroom socket, and sure these are small things, but they ate like acid on me.

Why her? Why so easy, so generous? What was she that I wasn't? What did she do to deserve it all so immediately? What had I done, or not done, to deserve the way he had treated me, the way he *was* treating me? The way I was forced to watch him reward her for nothing more than the apparently incredible luck of being different than me ... not being me, to be exact, just a younger, smarter model, who would show all the good from being with Dan and none of the scars.

He would – and did – reward her, in other words, for not having suffered alongside of him through the rough years, while punishing me for it. What's strange is that she wanted to punish me for it, too. Why? She hadn't been there. Why in the name of sanity was she jealous about missing those times? And make no mistake about it, she was. No matter what anyone says, Linda was as obsessed with me as I was with her.

She was jealous of every day I'd had with Dan that she hadn't, and it seems to me he was trying his hardest to make that up to her, and she was trying her hardest to make me pay for every missing day. The thing is that she wouldn't have wanted him then – only I had. Why did that make them both so mad at me all the time?

Dan had begun paying all her bills from 1983 onward with our money. Every cent Dan ever made was half mine, whether he believed that or not, and I guess he did, but he also knew it would play out differently because he told me once, "The law says you own it, Betts, but it doesn't say I have to give it to you. You try and get it. You just try!"

After my first trial, the one with the hung jury, a male juror told the press, "We only wondered what took her so long. A normal person would have killed that son of a bitch a lot sooner." Do you see why he might have said that, why I might have lost it and done exactly that? I don't agree that a normal person should kill someone, no matter what, but I wasn't normal by then, nor was it normal the way Dan treated me. We were extreme cases, maybe that's why people were interested in us, I don't know.

Here's an important thing, an insight maybe into how everything went so wrong. Dan knew I was conflict-phobic from my youngest days. I hated arguing and fighting over anything. I'd just walk away. There's another name for it – *angrophobia*. People that suffer from this pathetic condition usually have grown up with angry parents, and thanks to my mother that's me all over. Its downsides are that you will likely spend your life going out of your way to avoid conflict and become the type of passive person who always lets others take the lead, or you might find escape routes by cutting yourself off from others until you think they won't be angry anymore, which is what I did as a little girl by babysitting and taking on all those jobs. But, and here's the rub, anger is an unavoidable human emotion, and although many of us express anger in unhealthy ways – say by yelling at people or criticizing them all the time – it turns out that choosing not to express it is just as dangerous, if not more so. In fact I may be the poster-child for this.

I've learned, a little late in the day, that bottled-up feelings will generally turn inward over time, causing increased fear and hopelessness that lead to depression, putting you at risk of snapping and unloading all that self-hatred and rage on yourself and others in destructive ways. Like I said, I'm the poster child. There is even a TV

185

show called 'Snapped' now that featured me in one episode as a worst-case-ever scenario. So I'm not being a Diva here. I really am like a living billboard for not acting this way.

But this time I couldn't walk away, not from my children who wanted so badly to be with me. I lost on every money issue and kept slinking away in silent defeat, but for them I felt I had to stand and fight. Or I wanted to, but conflict-hating woman that I am, I fought back in every wrong way possible, i.e. I always had to wait until I snapped and then I retaliated in deranged ways, and if everyone thought I was a lunatic, including Dan and Linda, well kind of hard to blame them on that one.

With my kids, though, it really was my job to protect them, and, loon as I may have been, I was still the better of two evils, not that the courts recognized that. Dan was a physically and emotionally abusive alcoholic who didn't even like kids, yet they decided this was the guy that was the right primary parent for the children I loved more than life itself.

I put their safety and happiness first, while he never considered what was best for them. Over time, Dan bought a series of two-seater sports cars and his new house had no family room, no pool, no place for children to play and was located in an area where there were no other kids to play with. The children hated it there; it was an exclusively adult world. Whereas I maintained my house, my Chevy

186

Blazer and my pool specifically for when they came to visit. They loved being at my house, they loved me, and oh I loved them … love them.

Chapter 22

1985: STOP DRAGGING MY HEART AROUND

Before Dan destroyed me in court, he had worked to destroy me in private. Saint Patrick's Day wasn't the only time Dan had come around drunk, trying to be nice to me after he moved out.

That year, 1985, when I was still in love with my husband, and still lying to myself and other people about how we might reconcile, was as crazy-making a year as any that had preceded it, including all those years of his maliciously denying his relationship with Linda.

I never knew how I'd feel from one day to the next. Sometimes I almost convinced myself that I was glad he was gone, and for a minute or two I would be. But if I'm going to be totally straight here, I was in Hell.

The morning he left, I felt like I'd been hit by a car. I didn't know what to tell the kids and so I think I told them he'd be back after his "break." I didn't know what to tell our friends. Sometimes I needed support so badly I'd cry and say how scared I was and that I missed him; other times I'd tell anyone who would still listen that him moving out was the best thing that ever happened to me; and then I'd turn around and say that he would come home the minute his mid-life crisis was over.

188

I wasn't deliberately lying to anyone. At any given moment I might be thinking and feeling any one of those things, and Dan's actions weren't helping.

Dan and I were talking on the phone almost every day after he moved out, and even though he didn't come home after spending the night of St. Patrick's Day with me, I thought he might, and he did promise that we would spend our sixteenth anniversary together that April 12th. I bought a new dress (me and my new dresses!), did my hair, my nails, the whole thing. I was almost ready when he called late that afternoon and said he was sorry but he had to cancel, he was having dinner with "a bank teller about a case." I was really upset and by then I wasn't hiding things very well from the kids, so they saw me crying and swiping off my makeup.

I knew in my head that there was no bank teller, just his office girl – now girlfriend – telling him he'd better skip his anniversary dinner with me. I knew that, but then I didn't let myself know it, if you know what I mean. I was the stupidest person on earth for listening to him and letting him raise my hopes, but I'd been so stupid about Linda for so long already, what was a little more denial?

A few days after the anniversary dinner that didn't happen, Dan agreed to meet me for lunch to discuss matters relating to us, the kids and our future financial arrangements at the La Jolla Beach and Tennis Club. Dan told me he was sorry he had missed our anniversary and repeated his story about having to dine with a bank teller. I guess I'm pathetic, because even though I didn't believe him, I felt sorry for him. I thought maybe he was torn and confused about what he was doing and what he was going to do. He asked me to give him "more time." And I did because I wanted him to mean what he said and hoped that he was just taking time and space to think things over. I thought, if I didn't pressure him, and if he really was thinking things over, then he'd come to his senses.

From where I sat, we seemed to be the right choice. I still didn't understand any of it. Dan and I had struggled for so long and we'd made it. We had four beautiful and very young children who loved and needed us both, and I still thought we could have each other. I still loved him. I hated him sometimes as well, but I always, always loved him – we don't get a choice about that.

I told him all of this, and that if he came home we could go on, that I wouldn't even say anything about any of it. I was pathetic and obviously he thought so too.

He told people later that he *had* to keep lying to me because I was so "unstable" and he didn't know what I might do. But that was a lie, too. What Dan saw was that as long as I had the slightest hope that we could put our family back together again, I would just sit there with my head down and not get a lawyer and not ask questions, and that he could use the extra time I was giving him, while my head was

190

buried in the sand, to bury me for real.

In the next few weeks he would hang up on me when rats infested our rental house and I called him, hysterically begging for help. Then he broke the lease and forced us out of the rental house, and when I reacted to these things by dropping our kids off back at their home so I could go to New York – and, yes, also try to make Dan see he needed me – he just kept them and wouldn't give them back to me when I returned from my dad's 75th birthday.

Then he filed restraining orders to keep me out of my home on Coral Reef while he basically moved his girlfriend in with my children.

All of that was what he used the extra time I'd given him for. Before 1985 finished, though, he still had some ugly surprises left to hurt me with.

At the end of the summer of that horrible year, Dan filed for divorce and by then I was living in the house I'd bought as "our new family home," a very large old house that was basically a wreck. There was graffiti on the walls, it had mice and a yucky old stained shag carpet, and I didn't have any furniture and was sleeping on an air mattress – that is when I could sleep, because I'd never lived alone before and I was scared all the time, and already so upset and anxious I was becoming a permanent insomniac.

One of the things I was anxious about was that Dan had hired "nannies" for my kids who were basically street people, and I worried about my children all the time, especially my baby Rhett, who was almost always in tears. The so-called housekeepers must have been cheap, which would explain why Dan picked them, because they didn't play with my kids, or cook for them, or do anything at all, as far as I could see, besides watch TV. One day I showed up and found one of them wearing my favorite plaid shirt. When I asked her where she'd gotten it, she shrugged and told me that, "Dan said you weren't coming back and that I could take what I wanted."

However I think the "drunk dial" call was the worst. By the fall of 1985 I was really trying. I'd cleaned up a lot of the house and I had my new guy friends, Brad and Brian, and sometimes I had fun with them and could go whole hours without crying. But Dan must have had radar or something, because that November he decided to take the kids and Linda with him to the USC/Notre Dame football game on the twentieth anniversary of our first meeting there. I was trying hard not to think of this or to consider going there myself, so I had both Brad and Brian over at the house to play Scrabble with me and keep me company on the night of the game. The phone rang – it was Dan. He was calling from South Bend. He was totally drunk and he wanted to reminisce with me about how we'd met twenty years ago that night, how beautiful I used to be, and how much he used to love me.

What a jerk! It was so cruel of him.

The guys were listening to my end, so I told Dan to get off the phone and go find his office girl and stop bothering me. But that night, alone in bed, I felt sicker and hated myself more than I had at any time over the last two years. I felt so old, and ugly, and failed, and just … wrong. Didn't he understand that if I could have kept myself twenty and beautiful so he'd still love me, I would have done it? Talk about crazy time.

Dan was trying to drive me crazy with mixed messages from the start of 1983 and beyond, and he was doing an excellent job of it.

Chapter 23

PLAYING DIRTY

She who faces death by torture for each life beneath her breasts
May not deal in doubt or pity – must not swerve for fact or jest.
These be purely male diversions – not in these her honor dwells.
She the other Law we live by, is that Law and nothing else.
She is wedded to convictions – in default of grosser ties;
Her contentions are her children, Heaven help him who denies.
He will meet no suave discussion, but the instant, white hot wild
Wakened female of the species warring as for spouse and child.

Rudyard Kipling

194

I am a mama bear, my kids are my hot button, and Dan knew it. I didn't need physical possession of them, but I absolutely needed to know they were happy and well cared for.

They were not well cared for at Dan's house. They were not happy there at all.

Dan kept telling them and everyone else, "Your mother's sick," as always twisting things around so that he appeared to have done nothing at all and his ex-wife was just an insane crazy bitch who wanted him back at all costs. Oh my God! Dan hanging onto my kids, merely to use them as prisoners of our war to manipulate, control and hurt me – now that was sick.

The San Diego District Attorney's office has a tape of an illegally recorded phone conversation between my son, Danny, and me from Easter of 1987, which they introduced into court at both of my trials without the slightest right to do so. The call originated from Dan's house to mine, and in California you must have the consent of both parties for an audio recording to be admissible in court.

Dan knew the law, and I'd like to assume the D.A. knew it too, but in that tape went into both trials in blatant violation of a California Supreme Court ruling. Why my lawyer, Jack Earley, allowed this to happen, I shall never know.

Then those creeps had the nerve to play it again at my parole hearing in 2010, to show how angry and out of control I was. You bet I was angry. Every time Dan used and abused the kids as pawns and prisoners of war to hurt them and me, I went ballistic on him, finally quite literally. That is what he wanted, too; he wanted me to go nuts and then he'd sneak downstairs and secretly record the phones calls to prove what an insane freak I was. Same old, same old. He'd do something horrible and then twist it around and twist me up, and it always made me look bad, though I'll agree I never refused the bait, no matter how many times I ended up on the hook for it.

Here's the true scenario on the Danny call ... and bear with me because I get mad just thinking about it. Ugh!

I had an attorney at the time and she had arranged that I was to get the boys for a week-long Easter break from their school, Francis Parker. The boys were so excited to be spending a whole week at my house, just pure 'Mama time.' I had a calendar of planned activities on my fridge because they had been telling me for ages what they wanted to do while they were there and I didn't want to forget anything.

I had bought four hundred dollars' worth of groceries to have on hand so that I wouldn't have to waste a minute grocery shopping during their week with me, and I prepared all their favorite foods ahead of time and froze them for quick access. Doing all that in the days ahead of their visit had been great for me too. It almost felt like they were already there.

196

Rhett was my baby. I really loved him and he loved me right back, and he was so little still that he was able to show it. Every moment that we were together was precious to me … and to him too, I think. It was Rhett who had made a plan for when I picked them up at school for our Easter break. "Mom, be first in line!"

Rhett, 1984

Every day there was a long line of mothers in cars awaiting the release of their children from school. Some even arrived really early and just sat in their cars reading and waiting so that they could get

197

their kids and leave without being stuck in the slow-moving line forever. I had promised Rhett that, no matter what, I'd be first and he wouldn't have to wait.

When the big day finally came, they were excited and so was I. I was so sad and depressed without my children. They were my life, the only life I wanted. I didn't really care about anything else.

When I pulled up that afternoon to the school very early so that I could be first in line for Rhett, Dan was already there ahead of me, just pulling away from the curb in his MG. The boys were both crying and looking out the back window waving to me.

What? No!

I went after him, cut off his car and got out of mine, already crying. "What are you doing? We planned this ... the boys ... I have everything ready. We're –"

"I changed my mind."

I was shaking, crying and sick to my stomach. This was in 1987 and I was beyond the end of my rope, with no no idea if I could take a second more of this, let alone years.

When Dan got to his house, both the boys started arguing with him about coming over to mine. He told them that if they could get me to stop calling him names, he'd think about it.

Danny phoned me in good faith on Dan's orders, crying. He was only ten and thought he had to try to fix things, I guess. But Dan himself wasn't acting in good faith; he was being a total, sneaky bastard. Imagine using our already heartbroken little boy to trick his distraught mother and do his dirty work for him.

During the phone call, Danny was crying and I was crying, too. I was so furious at Dan and so sick of his crap. Did I call his father names? You bet I did ... every name in the book, and some they haven't written yet. What else could I do with my anger and frustration over the things he had done to us all, and *kept* doing to us all? By the time of that call he had sold our jointly-owned house out from under me, he had 'bi-fornicated' (*see 'bifurcated'*) our marriage, and buried me under so many elisor and e*x parte* actions and Orders To Show Cause that environmental groups should have been picketing his office for his cruel disregard to trees. We were legally divorced on paper but I had no settlement or property or custody agreement.

For Dan, though, it probably wasn't a personal attack on the boys. They were just collateral damage. He simply saw a chance to obtain something, whether legal or not, that could be used against me – and it has, for over two decades.

After my experiences with my Del Mar lawyer during 1987, I began to deteriorate very badly. She had charged me over one hundred thousand dollars and I had gotten nothing in return. Then she had quit in exasperation and frustration after Judge Joseph sentenced me to jail for calling Dan names. She had pointed out to Judge Joseph that the restraining orders I had violated by calling him names had expired years before and had not been renewed. The judge reviewed the orders, saw that she was right, and went ahead and sent me to jail anyway – and so she quit. He further wanted me to write a letter, apologizing. Over my dead body was I going to do that for trying to connect with my children by phone.

None of this was helped by Linda, who was obviously living with Dan at the time, taking perverse glee in blocking me from my speaking to my kids who had always had their own phone number and line, first when we all lived together, and then later at Dan's house. I only called my kids' number ever. I had no desire to call either Dan or Linda and subject myself to their cruelty as well as the inevitable follow-up barrage of contempt orders, restraining orders, process servers, elisors, orders to show cause, and a weekend in jail.

Bearing in mind that I was calling my children on their own phone line and that this was the sole means of communication I had with them, try to imagine what it was like to hear her voice on their answering machine. Why she did that I don't know, except that I'll give her this, it worked every time like a charm. I cussed her out each time I heard her voice on their line. She had no business on that machine whatsoever. She could only have been doing it to poke me in the eye and it played out (pardon my pun) so beautifully for her and

Dan in terms of giving them a 'solid reason' to hit me with a raft of orders and threats, couched in legalese.

I usually just said the same stupid thing: "It's not your job to answer my kid's phone. It's your job to answer the phone at Dan's office." Then I'd add some obscenity or other. She recorded every single one of my pathetic, flailing rants at her, and Dan loved it. It was a cat fight and over him, the hero of the hour, the man every woman wanted. He kept all of those tapes as an example of "Crazy Betty," his mad ex-wife, who couldn't stop, *wouldn't* stop, because she wanted him back, 'desirable Dan the ladies' man.'

Judge Joseph lectured me half angrily, half sadly, telling me I was "harassing" them, wounding them, and creating pain and suffering for them.

Really? I saw it rather differently.

From my "crazy" point of view, it seemed that they were doing everything they could to purposely anger and upset me so that they could turn around and say I was harassing them.

That Judge ended up being the one who finally gave Dan the order to "keep the girlfriend off the phone" in 1987, after which there were no problems with me and my kids communicating, and sadly for Dan, no more tapes for a while. He had plenty by then anyway.

Danny and Rhett, May 1989. They were always happy
and had fun when they stayed over at Betty's house.

But in 1989 they got married and Linda was no longer Dan's girlfriend – she was his wife – whereupon she considered Dan's home to be her home and his kids to be her kids, and the letter of Judge Joseph's order stated 'girlfriend,' not 'wife.' So about ten minutes after they returned from their honeymoon, she reverted right back to the same tactics she had used in '85, '86 and '87, and put her voice back on their answering machine.

Her first message was ostensibly geared for any calls the kids might get from their friends, and not to irritate me. It said, "Hi, we're back from Greece all tanned and rested. Please leave a message." I'll agree that at face value that seems fairly innocuous, but since none of her family or friends were ever going to call her on the kids' phone, I still believe to this day that she did those petty things to get to me. It seemed it wasn't enough for them just to have their fun and live their lives; if they weren't telling me about it, it wasn't happening for them, a sort of 'If a Pina Colada gets drunk at the bar and we don't tell Betty about it, did it really get drunk at all?'

Of course the real point of these games was to see what I would do so that they in turn could show me what they would do – OSCs, court orders, jail time etc. This part is very important, though, because those last threatening and harassing letters that I received on November 5th, 1989, contain transcripts of my predictable hysterical reactions to her resuming her old routine on the kids' phone.

You cannot play with people like that. You can't use a woman's children, let alone her feelings of loss and pain and humiliation and agony, to manipulate and control her. If they were right in telling everyone that I was "crazy," then why push me further? If they were wrong and I wasn't crazy yet, why try to make me that way. Aren't people who are genuinely crazy out of control and a danger to themselves and others?

And what about my kids? Why not try to keep from pushing me further off the edge if for no one else's sake but theirs?

This was in 1989 and "time heals everything," right? When they got married, I wasn't psycho about it the way everyone thinks. I wasn't happy, obviously – I don't think there is a person alive who doesn't feel a pang at the news their ex has remarried – but I was a little hopeful. I thought they would surely leave me alone then. I mean, what more was left for them to say or do?

I don't know what Linda thought I thought about any of it, but I do know that the marriage gave her an inflated sense of power. She had Dan and he was all hers, the prize, 'desirable Dan the heartthrob man.' It's that she believed I cared that is laughable. If I had ever wanted him back, and maybe in my loneliest moments I had, those moments were long gone by 1989. There were gallons of, no rivers of, bad blood between us by then. You couldn't have paid me ten million dollars to spend another hour, let alone a lifetime, with that drunken, cheating, abusive bastard, not by then.

Ever since Dan had left me, I had actually been doing okay in the non-abusive male companion area. I was a nice, happy, well-thought-of woman back in 1985, and I literally still thank God each night for the three men I spent time with who made me feel like a human being again and helped me get through my years of endurance. In a lot of ways they saved my life.

Each one of them was younger, taller, cuter and far kinder than Dan Broderick ever was or could be. We hung out, we played tennis and Scrabble, we went to the beach, and we golfed. We laughed and danced and watched the sunsets off of my deck. They didn't know Dan and so they were mystified by everything he was doing to me. Why wouldn't he just settle and let me go?

But, in a very sick way, Dan showed that he was never going to relinquish his control over my life. I'm not saying this to give anyone the idea that I thought that Dan still had feelings for me, beyond those of hatred and revenge; I'm saying it because it was obvious. He controlled my children, my house and my car. I was totally dependent on his monthly checks, and those same checks did not give me one iota of security. He would send them late and he would deduct "charges" and "fines" at his whim. He could, and did, go to court any day of the week, ex *parte* of course (meaning my presence was not necessary), and change the amount he was to send me for any reason he saw fit.

Nobody ever understood that I never got out from under his thumb, not ever. Those last letters were threatening me with jail and fines again.

That alimony check was all I had to live off. I had no cushion or savings, because somehow my half of the millions of dollars of community property we had amassed from 1969 to 1989 came to a grand total of $24,000. This figure was arrived at after Dan had subtracted Epstein Credits and deducted what I owed to *his* lawyers. Yes, you did read that right: I had to pay *his* lawyers out of *my* settlement. He also charged me for half the cost of his Harvard loans, which in court was couched as "our" student costs. Funny that I somehow owned a full fifty percent of our community debts but not one cent of our community assets. It doesn't take a math genius to see something was very badly wrong there.

Actually, by Dan's creative calculations, all of which the court backed up, I owed him many thousands of dollars in our divorce, but he decided to be patient about this and offered to let it slide without interest for the time being. However the proviso was added that if I ever did get the money from somewhere, he would have the right to come after it.

All this was decided inside sealed, secret, private courtrooms within a local legal system he had a lot of influence and control over. I might even say 'undue' influence and control over, but I won't because I don't want to sound like the same old "crazy, paranoid" woman that they knew back then.

Nope, I've seen the light. If I ever get out of here, I won't jaywalk in San Diego, or even walk and chew gum in San Diego. After all, I hear there are openings at Guantanamo Bay, and given the way my luck has gone so far … *eek!* Nope, let me just say this: If ever there was a place where justice for all was served, it's San Diego, and I'm so glad I have been able to live long enough to write about my long and proud journey inside this one-of-a-kind system that upholds

206

so well the best of our country's jurisprudence.

I shudder to think but is it at all possible that 'Dapper Dan the courtroom ham,' who got every judge that he ever asked for to preside over his medical malpractice cases, might have just greased the skids a little for his own trial? No, no it can't be. I feel terrible even suggesting this as a possibility. Clearly, as the parole board said, I'm still suffering from anger issues and I need to work to cleanse myself of such evil and counterproductive thoughts. Everything was handled in a professional, proper and above-board manner.

Above-board? Mmmm. Should the media have ever wanted to verify the facts, they would have discovered that the files had been sealed and that they would not have been able to gain access to them. Still, I guess Dan was right: I'm just paranoid.

Actually, Dan was so afraid the media would go to court and demand access to those files that he stole them. They mysteriously disappeared. 'Oprah' and '60 Minutes' were interested in this case back in 1987 as an example of one of the "Messiest Divorces in America." It was then that the files vanished. As for my reaction to this interest, well I told Oprah that I couldn't go on her show in 1987 because Dan would kill me if I went public with any of this. A newspaper tried to investigate the story and write about it, but Dan threatened to sue them and they knew he meant it. In fact the reporter said to me, "He'll do to us the same thing he's doing to you. He'll drag us through court, costing us a lot of money, and even if we can prove it's true, who cares, he'll have bankrupted us in the meantime."

So they, too, were afraid of Dan Broderick.

I was in such bad shape after the incident at Easter 1987 that I could barely function anymore. I was severely depressed and suicidal. I went to a psychiatrist for help. He said, "You don't need a psychiatrist as much as you need a lawyer."

His partner, Nelson Lewark, gave me a bunch of tests which established what I already knew: that I was very depressed and very anxious at the same time. He said, "Betty, imagine that you are a car engine with the gas pedal, which is your anxiety, pressed to the floor, and the brakes, which are your depression, pressed to the floor at the same time. What's going to happen to the engine? It's going to blow up."

I completely got what he was saying, but I couldn't fix the totaled car that I had become, and neither could he. He was nice, though, and it was a relief to have someone sympathetic to talk to.

I don't even remember 1988. By Christmas I was so suicidal and depressed that I could barely hold my head up and breathe. I was tired all the time but I couldn't sleep at all. I stopped going out because I could no longer pretend everything was okay. It wasn't. I'd lost all interest in everything. I wasn't the life of the party anymore and I knew if I went anywhere I'd just depress people by being around them. My three guy friends were still there, and they did everything they possibly could to bolster me up, but it was pretty much a hopeless task.

Kim and Lee were having teenage problems at Dan's house and he was handling them badly. The boys were desperate to be with me but I had no ideas left on how I could get them back with me, and no money left to try either. I missed the summer of 1985 – birthdays, holidays – and the fun of daily life was pretty much beyond me by then. 1985, '86, '87, '88 and most of '89 were 'beat down on me' time.

Christmas 1985 – first year apart with the children living with Dan

Dan used to say to the kids, "What's she going to do about her life? Just cry?"

Yep, that's pretty much what I did, and when I thought I was cried out, I found out I was wrong.

Somehow, and I don't even remember how, I got to have the boys for two straight weeks in the summer of 1989. We planned a car trip, like we had in 1983 when we were all still happy and together. Rhett was the cutest kid you ever saw. He had curly hair and he was totally energetic. He loved to water-ski and downhill ski. He'd been doing both since he was two years old.

That summer, at my house, he had seen on TV that you could snow ski in the middle of the summer at Whistler in British Columbia, Canada.

"Cool," I said, "let's go!"

So we did. We drove all the way from La Jolla to Whistler so that Rhett could snow ski in the middle of the summer and we had a fabulous time.

I loved my Suburban for a long trip. 'LODEMUP' – as it said on my license plate – was a lot of fun for us. We did everything on that trip: We camped alongside rushing rivers, we rode horses, we rafted, we hiked, we canoed, and my boys got to snow ski in the summer.

Whistler, 1989 – last trip together

Since I had them with me, I had scheduled appointments with lawyers and therapists to try and get them back before the start of the school year in September as it was important to them, and to me, that they start the new school year from my house. La Jolla had soccer teams and t-ball teams, and the scouts and the beach, and you had to sign up for everything in September. I had promised the boys I'd have them back by the start of school and so I tried yet another darn lawyer to make it happen,

My accountant flipped out on me. "Betty, what the Hell are you doing? You're throwing good money after bad and its money you don't have. You can't keep doing this."

I started crying and told her, "I don't care if it's my last cent. The boys want to be with me and I'm going to do everything possible to make that happen."

Besides, I didn't think I could lose. Dan never had anything to use against me as a parent and I was shocked when Judge Howatt awarded custody to Dan at the divorce trial in January of 1989. Why? There was no valid reason beyond him just not liking me and wanting to please Dan. The boys were unhappy living with Dan and I was a good mother. It made no legal, logical or common sense to leave the kids with him and Linda.

My new lawyer filed the papers to get us into court before school started. Hooray!

I had never even discussed, or considered, child support by that point. I didn't care about any money; I just wanted them home with me.

The big court day approached and Dan had it postponed without providing any reason to me or the boys. Remember, possession is nine tenths of the law. He had our boys and he was not going to let me get them. Why? Because then Dan Broderick would have lost his control over me once and for all. Whenever I had the kids with me, there was no reason to talk to him, call his house or go over there. I wanted nothing to do with Dan or Linda. They were living a life I had chosen to leave back in 1982 when I had started going to Al-Anon. I had had terrible heartbroken, jealous moments, obviously I had, but I didn't miss hanging out with good old Don and his new secretary / beard / wife. That was not a lifestyle I either aspired to or wanted but, as it turned out, that was always the lifestyle Dan had dreamed of while I had been picturing us doing this 'Joseph and Rose Kennedy' thing, maybe without the whores and the kids who got shot by lunatics … but you get my point. So I do kind of get it that Dan and I were never exactly on the same page, or even in the same library, so to speak.

September came and went, and Dan kept putting off the hearing until "sometime in October," making it that the boys couldn't start the school year from my house for another year. When October came around, he put the hearing off until December. I was furious at my lawyer for allowing Dan to get away with that. That was the same thing he had done with the divorce settlement, delay, delay, delay, while he had full possession of everything and I had no custody over the children or financial freedom of movement at all, but this attorney was new to our case and had no idea of what I had been through before he came along.

Ironically by then I had become the desperate, crazy person that Dan and Linda had always said I was. I was so tired of his legal bullshit, time after time, year after year. He was killing me by inches, honestly he was. I felt so bad for my boys. I had promised them that if they went to all these appointments during the summer, I would go to court and get them back ... and I had failed them, again.

I was a woman of my word. If I said I was going to do something, I did it. People, mostly my kids, could count on me, but I had failed them.

Then it was November of 1989, my birthday, and I was turning forty-two. I had taken pills and slit my wrists on my birthday in 1983 because of how badly Dan had been treating me, and here we were six years later and he was still at it. I'll never understand – and believe me, I've tried – why he couldn't just leave me and the kids and go off with his secretary, like so many other men had, and still do, after they have reached forty. Why did he need to destroy me and our family on his way out? It seems that somehow only by applying this total-war, scorched-earth policy could he show that he had been forced to leave, that he wasn't a jerk, just a man trying to survive impossibly trying circumstances and that he was not having an affair with his office assistant while he was still living with and married to me. He actually thought he had got away with convincing everyone that his wife was so "sick" that he had to raise the children all alone, or alone with Linda and a stream of housekeepers, anyway.

Dan was a master manipulator and a liar; it's what made him a great attorney. He lied for a living and he was very adept at it. The other guy, no matter if the other guy was a wife or one of his own children, was always at fault in his worldview.

I cannot leave this 'playing dirty' theme without sharing the details of what went on at my parole hearing in 2010.

If you are reading this book, then I'm guessing you know a great deal of my story and so you are aware that I was convicted of second degree murder for the deaths of Dan and Linda Broderick on November 5, 1989. Second degree murder, at least in California, means that it was determined by the jury that there was no premeditation, and there wasn't. I reacted to the latest threats and provocations from the two people who became in turn my victims on that last day.

Here are the verbatim transcripts of the letters I read when I got up that morning. The District Attorney has always said that they were non-offensive letters, telling me I was going to get my boys back. I'll let you decide for yourselves. These letters arrived forwarded to me in one packet from my then custody attorney Walter Maund:

DANIEL T. BRODERICK
A PROFFESSIONAL LAW CORPORATION
ATTORNEY AT LAW
610 WEST ASH STREET, SUITE 800
SAN DIEGO, CALIFORNIA 92101

TELEPHONE (619) 239-3344
DANIEL T. BRODERICK
ROBERT VAAGE
KATHLEEN CUFFARO

November 1, 1989

Walter Maund, Esq,
707 Broadway, Suite 1700
San Diego, CA. 92101

Re: Broderick Child Custody/Visitation

Dear Mr. Maund:

I have your letter of October 27, 1989.

216

*After the depositions of Dr. DeVoss and Dr. Nelson,
you proposed to Mr. Broderick that there be a trial
period during which custody of Danny and Rhett
would be modified by stipulation to substantially
increase the amount of time Respondent spent with
them. You proposed that any agreement worked out
along these lines contain a provision to the effect that
the modified custody arrangement would terminate
immediately upon a violation by Respondent of
existing court orders of the terms of the modification
agreement. You indicated that the agreement could
contain a provision that it could not be used in any
subsequent proceedings before the court. You told Mr.
Broderick you wanted to discuss the specific terms of
the matter with Dr. de-Voss (sic), Dr. Nelson and
Respondent and told him you would send him a
written proposal for his consideration.*

*As you obviously know, the proposal contained in your
letter of October 27 bears little or no resemblance to
what you and Mr. Broderick have discussed. First it
appears to involve a permanent modification of Danny
and Rhett. There is no mention whatsoever of a trial*

217

period. Second there is no provision for the automatic termination of the new custody arrangement if the Respondent violates an existing court order or the terms of the agreement itself or if she further involves Danny or Rhett in her pathological obsession with their father and his wife. Third, there is no mention of any provision to the effect that the agreement may not be used in any subsequent court proceedings in this matter.

Walter Maund
November 1, 1989

Page Two

Mr. Maund, I really wonder whether you are sincere about trying to work out a shared custody arrangement on a trial basis. There are many other fundamental problems with your proposal. Unless and until you reorient yourself to the whole point of these negotiations (negotiations that you initiated I might add), I don't see any reason to go into them. I suggest you try again to come up with a proposal that is consistent with what you and Mr. Broderick have discussed. It should also reflect the child support payments Respondent may be seeking during the trial period.

I look forward to the early receipt of your revised proposal.

Sincerely yours,

KATHLEEN CUFFARO

That was the first of the two letters from Dan's associate, Kathleen Cuffaro, that I read. The following is a verbatim copy of the second. Please note my scrawled response on the bottom. This constituted my suicide note.

DANIEL T. BRODERICK

A PROFFESSIONAL LAW CORPORATION

ATTORNEY AT LAW

610 WEST ASH STREET, SUITE 800

SAN DIEGO, CALIFORNIA 92101

TELEPHONE (619) 239-3344

DANIEL T. BRODERICK

ROBERT VAAGE

KATHLEEN CUFFARO

October 27, 1989

Walter Maund, Esq,

707 Broadway, Suite 1700

San Diego, CA. 92101

Re: Broderick v. Broderick (sic)

Dear Mr. Maund:

Enclosed please find a verbatim transcript of just a few of this week's obscene messages left on my client's

220

answering machine by Respondent. You will note that all of these messages are directed at the children. Needless to say, my client and his wife are very upset that this type of behavior is still occurring, not to mention the effect it has on his sons. I am writing to elicit your help in getting Respondent to stop this offensive conduct.

You should know that since Judge Howatt's final ruling of January 30, 1989, Respondent has committed at least 20 separate acts of contempt for which we have documented proof. Although my client would prefer to avoid filing contempt charges against Respondent, he is prepared to do so if her odious behavior does not stop immediately. As you may know, Respondent was ordered to pay $26,000 in penalties and was sentenced to 25 days in jail for various contempt violations in the past. I firmly believe that if my client and I are forced to seek the court's assistance in enforcing the restraining orders in existence, another jail sentence will be imposed.

The Brodericks would like Respondent to know that

the phone ringers have not been turned off on the phones in their home since the first day school started. Perhaps you should also tell her that every morning the boys feed the dogs in their backyard and therefore cannot hear the phones ringing at that time. This is where they were Wednesday morning, she called approximately 15 minutes after the boys had already been picked up for school by the bus.

Walter Maund, Esq.
October 27, 1989

Page Two

Finally, I find Respondent's actions completely inconsistent with the contentions of her psychotherapists that her emotional disturbances and mental disease are improving. The contrary appears to be the case.

Very truly yours,

KATHLEEN CUFFARO

222

Cc: Gary DeVoss Ph.D.
Gerald Nelson, M.D.

I can't take this anymore

1.   Linda Kolkena the cunt interfering with what little contact I have left with my children. She's been doing it for years and we've litigated it continuously.

2.   Constant threats of court, jail, contempt, fines etc. Which is very scary to me and us, Walter. What is the point if I always lose?

3.   Them constantly insinuating I'm crazy.

Then I attempted a futile last answer to Kathleen Cuffaro, Dan's kindly associate.

11/5

Dear Ms. Cuffaro,

Your verbatim transcripts of the calls to my sons are of no use to anyone, but to me, to show the court's endless abuse I suffer at the hands of the mentally deranged Mr. Broderick.

The issue of my being able to return my children's phone calls has been litigated ad-nauseam, since 1985!! Judge Tony Joseph and Judge Thos. Murphy ordered my ex-husband to keep his office cunt off the kid's telephone line. By allowing her to tamper with the line it is Mr. Broderick and not I who should be in contempt.

As everyone in San Diego knows, Mr. Broderick has used his political influence as President of the Bar

Assoc, his Harvard Law Degree and his endless, influential friends to abuse, and batter and severely abuse me and our four innocent children.

I am really sick of being his victim.

If anyone in the family has a mental disease it sure is him.

These letters were not submitted in either of my trials. Instead, what the jury heard was the D.A.'s inference and Kathleen Cuffaro's testimony and it went a little like this: "Mr. Broderick was offering Mrs. Broderick sole custody of the boys. That's all those letter were. There was nothing at all in there to cause her to lose it," followed by some sighs and head shaking, *crazy Betty, Betty, Betty, Betty.*

The District Attorney tried twice, and failed twice, to get a first degree conviction. Dan's brother, Larry, wanted me to get the death penalty, but that was never an option in the case. Ironically, judges' discretion came into play again. When the judge chose to give me two separate convictions for one terrible moment in time, he saved my life and damned me to an eternity in here as well. His discretion was not used to benefit me, and it hasn't, but it did, I suppose, save my life, assuming, that is, that a jury would have found me guilty of first

225

degree murder and then given me death in the penalty phase. The reason he did it is because, by making it two separate cases and not one, he could double the fifteen-to-life sentence should there be a second degree conviction.

My case should have had concurrent and not consecutive sentences because this was one incident with two victims, but you can't argue with a judge's discretion, so I got fifteen-to-life, plus fifteen-to-life, plus an added two years for the use of a firearm.

Chapter 24

INSIDE OUT

There are certain things you have to do to be found suitable for parole after your time is up. The whole system inside prison is built on the premise that convicts are addicts with no education and job skills. They want you to attend '12 Step' groups and get a G.E.D., and learn a vocation, so that when you get out you can obtain a job upon release.

They want you to have support letters and parole plans, and in 2010 I was ready to leave. I had met and exceeded all the requirements, and I had served my sentence – you get three months off of each year if you don't get any discrepancy write-ups.

In 2010, Larry Broderick was still as angry at me as he was on the day of the killings in 1989. I wasn't angry anymore, not at anyone. For me it was over and done with, and I thought we could all get on with what was left of the rest of our lives. I had paid my debt to society, and my children and grandchildren would never have had to come to see me in prison again, but Larry is on a mission to make sure I die in here. He was extremely upset that the death penalty was not on the table during either of my trials, but I think he has become pragmatic in our old age and decided that 'death by denials' will work out okay for him.

Prior to my parole hearing he rallied both families and all of Dan's legal friends to write letters protesting my release. That's understandable. I hurt a lot of people when I killed Dan and Linda. They each had families and friends, none of whom had a clue about the events that led up to that fateful day.

I've always wondered if their knowing the truth would have changed things or not, or if even attempting to tell them would have made them angrier. That's the thing, you have to learn to be Christ-like in prison for the parole board and you have to forgive thirty-times-thirty.

If I had said to Dan and Linda's family and friends, "Yes, God yes, I'm so sorry I killed them, but they were killing me," then wouldn't that have only served to make them madder at me? To defend a single one of my actions, I have to tell about an event that caused me to act out, and that means saying something about either of them, or both of them, that no one wants to hear.

They are dead, and the beloved dead become sacred to people. It doesn't matter who they were in life; death washes us all with sainthood. And, see there, even what I just wrote looks provocative. But if I say that I was always simply evil, or crazy, or both, then no one in their right mind should let me out, and that's sort of Larry's argument. "Betty Broderick is a danger to society." So what should I say? What should I do?

I know what some people think: that saying I'm sorry means I'm sorry I'm in prison and not that I killed two people. They're wrong and they are right, because, of course, I'm sorry I'm in prison – everyone and anyone in their right (or wrong) mind is sorry to be in prison – but I'm also sorry that I ended two lives.

The thing is, though, I feel like I'll never be free unless I say that I ended the lives of two people who never did me any harm, and I can't say that. And I can't say I was hopelessly insane because the court said otherwise, so I don't know what to say or feel anymore, and that's awfully reminiscent of the six years prior to the killings.

Back to the playing dirty portion of my parole hearing, it seems the D.A. brought a packet of sealed / secret / confidential letters along with him. Here we go again, with sealed and secret … and might I say *crooked*? I'm the most public and secret woman in America simultaneously. That's some trick!

Remember, the D.A. wasn't the only lawyer on my parole hearing: All Dan's friends are lawyers and they know what needs to be said "legally" to find me to be a "present danger" to society and to keep me in here until I'm taken out in a body bag, by which time, presumably, I won't be able to hurt anyone else, though just think about the ghost sightings they'll be able to talk about down at Reidy O'Neil's. Who needs a pink elephant when you can regale your friends with seeing Betty Broderick floating above your bed?

229

Don was around, and he's even angrier than Larry, probably because, unlike Larry, he simply loved and misses Dan and didn't owe him any money ... but I digress.

They knew anger alone wouldn't keep me in here. There's no one who has ever been in prison who hasn't made a lot of people angry at them for one thing or another, but crime is a growth industry, so they still have to let people out. After all, we're all being rehabilitated here, unless you are like me, apparently beyond all rehabilitation or hope. So since anger wasn't going to do it, they had to claim that they are all living "in fear for their lives if I am let out."

Eek! *Serial Grandma, Big Bad Betty, Betty the Boogeywoman.* I can see their point, too. After all, I'm not a pretty sight without my support garments these days, and I've long felt that, should I be released, no ice cream parlor would be safe from me. I love ice cream and I've heard that about a thousand new flavors have been created since I've been in here.

I'm certainly not going to suggest that there are lawyers in this world who have no qualms whatsoever about lying to advance their cases. That would make me sound paranoid and crazy, like Dan used to say I was. Nope, all lawyers are the heart and soul of integrity and virtue ... and that's my story and I'm sticking to it. I will say that none of them had the courage to put a single name on their letters or to show their faces at the parole hearing, though that may have less to do with crooked games than their very natural fears of me coming after them, stealing their Hagen Daaz, and then doing away with them, never mind that I never met any of them and wouldn't recognize them from Adam.

They handled it just right and there wasn't a coward or liar among them.

I had a very favorable psychiatric report done by psychologists for the California Department of Corrections and Rehabilitation which puts me in the low risk category, and that means you can't do better than that, yet the parole commissioner, who I think was heavily influenced by Larry Broderick, found me to be a danger to society and gave me the maximum possible denial of parole – fifteen years until the next hearing – which is more time than receiving another murder charge. He was fired shortly thereafter, but Larry had gotten his wish, and then some, by that time.

No woman in the entire prison system has ever been given a fifteen year denial of parole. Everyone I spoke to was shocked. I had been gang-raped, again. Before that hearing I had gotten over being angry at anyone anymore, but since then I've been angry all over again because it was *déjà vu,* it's a revival of every ugly losing moment in what seems to still be Dan Broderick's justice system. That's the one where the laws and the truth hold no sway over the dirty politics and the sweet little club that is the San Diego Bar

Association.

Speaking of the Bar Association, there must have been a few dozen toasts raised the night after my parole hearing, accompanied no doubt by a Capella round or two of 'Danny Boy.' It paints a moving picture, doesn't it?

There's nothing in my record that would justify a denial of any length, much less fifteen years. I can file appeals in court, but they have to be filed in San Diego courts. That's where the portrait and memories of the great Dan Broderick are, and where the award is given yearly. Yup, the annual Daniel T. Broderick Memorial Award Dinner is a much-anticipated event. The award, which has been presented since 1990, is to honor the lawyer who best represents the highest conduct in civility, professionalism and integrity. There's also a shrine to him at the San Diego Bar Association Headquarters and the main meeting room is named after him.

Each year a group of his friends meet at his grave and sing 'Danny Boy' and pour Irish whiskey on his plot. I imagine he likes that. The media covers this magnificent event each year. Personally, I'm offended that no one has cared enough to build at least a smaller version of the Lincoln Memorial in his honor, or to enact an eternal flame over his grave, and why not a rendering of his likeness, say on the San Bernardino Mountains, à la Mount Rushmore?

It seems that for those who maintain Dan's shining memory, he is their lodestar, a sort of secular Messiah, the best person they ever met, and one who represents all that they could aspire to be.

The District Attorney's made-for-TV movies are still shown constantly and I wonder who reaps the financial benefits from them, since no one I know, least of all our daughter Lee, has ever made a cent from exploiting this tragedy, and brother Larry is quick to threaten to sue anyone who dares to say anything in support of me, even Barbara Walters. No, really. When '20/20' covered the case, Barbara Walters said, "You know, I would never condone murder, but in this case I don't know ..." and Larry tried to sue her for that. I'll assume that he will sue me for this, but, and sorry to go to the clichés here, you can't get blood (or ice cream) out of a turnip, or out of an older woman who is growing older everyday as she waits to die in prison.

Chapter 25

LAST LETTERS

I can set the scene for what happened on that day, however I hate to ruin this day by going there mentally. It's a beautiful day today here at the California Institution for Women in Chino-Corona, California. The sun is shining, the birds are chirping in the tree outside my window, the one I can see the sunset from every evening.

I have a great roommate. We get along so well, and we cook and laugh and play Scrabble together. I'm well liked and well treated here, by the staff and the inmates alike.

I don't smoke or drink or do drugs in here, because I didn't do any of that stuff on the outside either, and those are not among the things I miss.

I'm still a Mom and a teacher in here, just as I was out there. I mentor young girls and help them with their legal work and getting their G.E.D.s. I am treated equally and respected by black and white and Hispanic women because I've never been prejudiced or partial to any race or kind of people, and the women who meet with and interact with me recognize that.

I am basically happy in here. I'm safe and there's a kind of freedom in that, and in knowing what to expect each day. I talk to and see my children and grandchildren. I suppose I live in a gated community, like lots of seniors do, because, in an odd way, I have maids, cooks, gardeners and even chauffeurs if I need to go somewhere. Free rent and no taxes, free food, laundry services, wardrobe consultants, along with a free wardrobe and medical. Dental and counseling services are all included.

I'll tell you the story of my twenty-five years of rehabilitation in the California Department of Corrections and Rehabilitation, and it's kind of funny because it's all true.

When I arrived at the prison in 1992, I had a college degree, a teaching credential, and, hilariously, a decorator's license and a real estate license. These things were not objects of admiration around here because, evidently, I needed to be rehabilitated to the standards of the CDCR.

I had no idea what it would be like. I'd never known anyone who had served time in prison, and so what I knew, if anything, was based on what I'd seen on TV and in movies, which is pretty much true for every American. I had zero idea how to act. We all want to fit in wherever we are and so I tried to fit in here.

The first thing I learned to do was to be a 'hooker.' Yes, Siree, they were all making these really hideous hooked rugs, so I ordered a few and got to work. I made a tiger, an eagle, and an American flag one, and a Christmas tree skirt.

When the kids came for our week-long family visit, I proudly presented them with these horrible creations. It was funny.

The next thing I learned was how to be a 'stripper.' Yep, they gave me a job as a porter. When I had gone to Classification and they had asked me what I wanted to do, I said I didn't want to work, that I was depressed and sick and needed to acclimate. They weren't too amused and said, "You have to have a job."

I said, "I thought enforced labor only existed in Chinese prisons."

I'm so stupid! Anyway, that's how I became a porter.

For my new job I was given a big machine, the likes of which I had never seen, and I was taught how to strip the floors. I really liked that job, and I liked all the girls I met in prison. They were very nice to me because they had heard my story before I got there and felt sorry for me.

Not long afterwards I was moved to the California Institution for Women here in Chino-Corona. I was very comfortable working for doctors and nurses and dentists and psychologists, and I got assigned as a front office receptionist, which I loved. The Mental Health department was in a trailer at that time, so I was a 'trailer trash' employee for a while. I liked working there so much.

Putting in so many hours at my desk there without taking breaks, though, caused my lower back to start hurting a lot. I had a bulging disc at the C5, which created terrible pain down my psychotic nerve.

Yes, I said 'psychotic.' Other people may have sciatica and sciatic nerves, but I always said mine was 'psychotic,' just for laughs. Anyone who has ever known me knows that I love to tell jokes and have fun with people. I'll do most anything to get a laugh out of someone, if I can. During the divorce years I didn't have anything to laugh or joke about, and it felt good to become my old self again.

One day my back hurt really badly and I walked over to the clinic to ask for a pain killer or a muscle relaxer. There was a guy sitting there reading a paperback book, and he asked me what I was there for. He was not a nurse or a doctor; he was a physical therapist. I told him my back was killing me and he said, "Come on in. I'll fix you right up."

I had had a wonderful chiropractor back in La Jolla who could, and did, fix me right up anytime my back hurt, and we don't have chiropractors in prison, but I thought a physical therapist might work too.

He told me to lay face down on the table. He did not have my x-rays or my file, and I didn't have a scheduled appointment with him. He was just doing this as a nice gesture. He stepped on a pedal, which forced my back to bend. At that point he badly ruptured the disc at C5 and seriously injured the nerve root. I could not move my left foot. I had never been paralyzed before and I was scared that I would never walk again. When I finally saw the prison doctor and told him how I couldn't move my foot, he said. "You know, I saw those movies about you."

What? What about my foot?

He offered me a 'Motrin and a Lay-In.' That's the prison panacea for every ailment.

I told him, "I don't need your Motrin or your lay-in. What about my foot?"

Now I was in even worse pain in my back, and I had tears streaming down my face, so he referred me to another prison doctor who told me, "You've got a virus in your foot."

What? Oh My God. Who are you ... what kind of medical school did you go to? This is Neurology 101.

Stupidly again I shared my opinion with him that he was an idiot, and I went out in the hall and told the girls who were waiting that he was an incompetent quack. I told him, "Doctors like you made my ex-husband a wealthy man."

He asked me, "What do you want?

I said, "I want you to fix my foot."

He offered me a Motrin and a lay-in. So now I was a 'crip,' and I had to go into the Program Office and register as a 'Gang Member' for disabled prisoners.

The next doctor who asked me what I wanted for my foot, I said, "I want Viagra, because its floppy and I can't get it up." It made sense

238

to me, and who knows, it might have worked better than a Motrin and a lay-in.

It took years before they finally got me out for back surgery.

So now that I'm a 'crip,' I walk slowly and I'm in a lot of pain every time my left foot hits the ground. One evening I was going to church and I was walking up the metal ramp to enter the building. My floppy foot caught and I fell. I grabbed onto the metal hand railing to break my fall. I hit the railing so hard that it left a sharp indented crack in my head. I was so thankful that I didn't break my teeth that I didn't even care that I was now a 'crackhead.' There are lots of us in prison.

Later, we established a vegetable garden on the grounds and that was the best things that ever happened at C.I.W. It was a lot of hard work but it got inmates of all ages and colors and backgrounds out working and having fun together. We've derived a lot of pleasure and a sense of accomplishment from that garden, not to mention all the great fresh vegetables we get to eat.

College students from the Claremont College came in and brought the material and plants and seeds. One of them was from Bronxville, so we struck up a great friendship. We worked the garden on weekends. I used to get into mud-wrestling matches with the hose on Sunday. You can spell that 'hoes,' 'hos,' or 'hose.'

I'd come home covered in mud from wrangling with it, and so

now I'm a 'mud wrestler' as well as a 'stripper,' 'hooker,' 'trailer trash,' 'gang member' and 'crackhead,' and so you see what the department of Corrections and Rehabilitation can do for you?

People told me, "Oh Betty, you should take that to the Parole Board."

Of course I wouldn't. They aren't famous for their enjoyment of humor up there, though, as it turns out, I couldn't have done any worse if I had made it into a one-woman comedy stand-up show.

I've already told you that I'll do anything to avoid re-living the events of that day, and I guess you might have already gathered that from my little 'how I spent my summer vacation' tales about the last twenty-five years.

You see, there's nowhere as bad as that day and the ones that preceded it, and it's terrifying to go back there again. At least that's what it feels like.

But, okay, no more jokes or stories ...

I was very mad at my lawyer, who was a very sweet guy, for allowing Dan to postpone the custody hearing again to "sometime in December." There wasn't even a firm date in December. Half the school year would be over by then and the boys and I would miss Halloween and Thanksgiving at the least.

My lawyer, Walter Maund, wrote a legal letter to Dan, proposing a new custody arrangement where the kids would live with me and have visitation with him. No money was mentioned.

Dan, via his associate Kathleen Cuffaro, wrote a snotty reply and resorted to his old tricks of 1985 and '86 by referring to the tapes Linda had made of me, cursing her out for being on my kids' phone line again.

I had already been down this road before and my earlier experiences hadn't built up any resilience or tolerance – quite the opposite. I was shell-shocked and battered from years of Dan and Linda's ceaseless legal battering.

And here it was again, *delay and distract*. Remember, I had been depressed and not sleeping for a long time, and that was still true, if not worse, during the renewed custody negotiations.

The boys were with me for the weekend. I don't remember if I got the mail out of the mailbox on Friday or Saturday that last weekend. I always got a lot of mail and it really doesn't matter when I got it because I threw most of it onto the kitchen counter. I wasn't planning on dealing with it until Monday when the boys left.

Brad was there, too, that weekend. Brad often stayed at my house, and I encouraged it because I really hated being there all alone.

I went to bed early because I was always tired. I knew it was from the depression, but that didn't do anything to make me less tired.

I had been in this weird state for a few years, where I could never sleep at night because I was so anxious. So I'd get up and wander around the house, try to read, couldn't concentrate, hit the refrigerator and stuff something into my mouth, try to sleep again, but not be able to because I was anxious about how fat I was. Then I'd get back up, wander around, turn on the TV, usually eat more, lie down, and get up again. So, during the day, I was in this exhausted fog, but I never wanted to try and sleep during the days because I kept hoping that, if I didn't, I could sleep at night, and I wanted very much to sleep at night because I dreaded the nights

242

I had hoped to get some sleep that night in particular because we had plans to go to Tijuana the next day. That was what Danny and Rhett wanted to do. Brad was planning on going sailing, as he often did on the weekends, so those were the plans – no problem.

I woke up early. I put coffee on and went out to get the newspaper from the walkway. I came back in and noticed the legal letter amid the rest of the mail. I opened it because the boys were asleep and I had time to read it.

And then bottom fell out of my world.

I started reading the threats and ultimatums, and the transcribed tapes and Dan's terms which were 'Subject to termination' at his whim again, always. He was threatening jail and fines, knowing full well that if I missed one house payment I'd lose the house.

He was trying to force me out of the house so he could then go back to court and reduce my monthly check, as he had already attempted to do. Not being able to reduce his monthly payments to me was the sole initiative that Dan had been denied so far and he wasn't going to let it stand. He had to have all and me nothing, or he wasn't winning at all. He was never going to let things rest until I was left with not one thing from our lengthy marriage, especially not our children, until I was finally reduced to the homeless, talking-to-myself, bag lady he and Linda saw me as. They weren't going to stop.

Why they needed my complete destruction before they could be

243

truly happy, I don't know, but surely they did. None of what Dan did was justifiable or necessary. He was a sick man. He was making so much money by then that what he paid me must have amounted to less than one of his monthly trips with Linda, or a clothing bill. He didn't need to cheat me out of everything, but he could and he did. Abuse of power is the most frightening and destructive form of abuse.

I completely fell apart. I didn't know what to do. I didn't want to go back to court, and back to jail, and I didn't want my boys on a trial basis. I knew exactly what that meant: Dan would be my judge and jury, and I knew how that would go – an endless Salem witch trial.

You see, he had another surefire trick to get me to break his restraining orders, besides Linda's voice on the answering machine. My support check was always late. Sometimes it came on the 3rd, sometimes on the 9th. I had begged the judge to order Dan to set up an automatic payment, but that request was denied.

I'd start to panic about paying the mortgage and I'd ask the kids to ask Dan because I was too afraid to call him directly, and so I knew what the 'involving Danny and Rhett in your client's pathological obsession with my client' portion of one of the letters meant.

I was so tired of all of it, and here were these new letters saying it's not only not going to end, it's going to ramp up again ... get ready. But I couldn't. There wasn't anything left in me to do this for another six years, or, by that point another six hours.

244

Standing in the kitchen that morning I could see no end to it all … not a single light at the end of the tunnel. I recalled his, "This will never be over" threat, and Linda telling everyone in town, "We're going to use the courts to drive her crazy."

Well, they had. It had worked out perfectly for them.

I had to make it stop. I could not live one more day like this, waiting for his next 'Gotcha!' I just couldn't stand it. I felt like I had failed my kids and I had nothing left to live for.

Dan had wanted to drive me to this moment. Dan and Linda had worked very hard through the previous six years to bring us all to that day.

I'd bought a gun months before. I bought it on the day that Linda and her sidekick Sharon Blanchett entered and robbed my home of my diary while I was at work.

The gun was under the seat in the locked Suburban, because the boys were visiting and I didn't want them to find it and touch it. I decided to go down to the beach to put a bullet in my head. Anything was better than this and I had to make it stop somehow.

While I was in the car I heard Danny's voice clearly speaking in my head, "Well, that's real smart, Mom. Now we're stuck with him."

That's what sent me to Dan's house to ask him one more time to give me my kids and leave me the Hell alone.

I had the gun that would force them to listen to me.

It was important to me that I get to the phone before they called the police and had me hauled off again. I needed them to hear me out, then they could do the usual, but they would have heard, and maybe it could change things.

Obviously I was not in my right mind. I wasn't even in a crazy person's right mind. I was disassociating and imagining scenarios that could never come to pass. I was no longer seeing or thinking clearly. This is what it feels like to go insane.

I had, I was.

Linda came up and lunged at me as soon as I stepped one foot in the doorway to their bedroom. I was startled and already hysterical, and I emptied the gun. I didn't change my own position from where I stood or move the gun around. I just fired from where I stood and I think I was screaming the whole time – the whole time was a second, though.

They both moved in opposite directions simultaneously. It really was a second. To empty a five-shot gun in a panic takes less than one second. That's from the F.B.I. statistics on the Reagan shooting, so it is true.

It can happen. It did.

I really did not go there to shoot or kill Dan and Linda. I had no need to hurt anyone, but I had a desperate need to make it stop. I just couldn't live another day under such suffocating and paralyzing stress and fear of what was coming next.

I couldn't breathe normally and I couldn't sleep. I had no life and no freedom, and everything I did was subject to Dan's will or mood, and his next nasty gram of choice.

Since he totally controlled my children, my home and my money, he still controlled me, and continued to do so years after he walked out. I could not live under his thumb anymore. He was crushing me like a bug, and he knew it.

Killing them would not fix anything. Killing me would, because that was always my go-to answer as to how to escape his cold-hearted abuse.

That's what I tried in 1973 and in 1983, and that was my answer in 1989. To kill myself, not him. Just me. And to end it once and for all. Because, as I wrote on the note I left that morning, "I just can't stand this anymore."

I had no idea Dan was hit. I went around the bed to get the phone. Dan put his hands up, like in the movies, and said to me clear as day, "Okay, okay, you got me."

He thought I was going to shoot him again.

I grabbed the phone and ran out of there. I laid rubber in the street. I thought he was chasing me.

I immediately turned myself in and told the whole truth about everything. I was more afraid of Dan catching me than I was of the police. They would protect me from him.

I never went home again. The lights were on and the coffee was ready. The doors were open and my boys and Brad were inside asleep.

This story can go on and on, about jail, and court and prison, and I've got some interesting and entertaining tales to tell, but they will have to wait for another book.

It's 2014 and I am sixty-seven years old. I've spent more than twenty-five years in jail on this case. I should be getting out of here one day, at least I hope so, unless Larry gets his wish and I die in here. I have no control over that and so I try not to dwell on it much.

In the end, I think I've had a wonderful life. I lived my dreams and I think regrets are a waste of time for people. You can't go back and change the past. There are no real-life time machines. No, this isn't the life I planned, obviously, but it's the life I have, so I will continue to embrace it go forward in love and peace. It's the best any of us can do and I'm going to keep trying my best.

Love and peace to all of you, too.

Betty.

Betty's 60th birthday with Danny, Rhett, their wives and children

9 781511 518628